THOUGHTS
ON
EDUCATION

THOUGHTS ON EDUCATION

Dr. S. Sabu
Ismail Thamarasseri

KANISHKA PUBLISHERS, DISTRIBUTORS
NEW DELHI-110 002

KANISHKA PUBLISHERS, DISTRIBUTORS
4697/5-21 A, Ansari Road, Daryaganj
New Delhi-110 002
Phones : 2327 0497, 2328 8285
Fax : 011-2328 8285
E-mail: kanishka_publishing@yahoo.co.in

Thoughts on Education
First Published 2010

ISBN 978-81-8457-183-7

PRINTED IN INDIA

Published by Madan Sachdeva for Kanishka Publishers, Distributors, 4697/5-21A, Ansari Road, Daryaganj, New Delhi-110 002, Typeset by Sunshine Graphics, Delhi, and Printed at Rajdhani Printers, Delhi.

Preface

The roots of present education embedded in the past. The future of it is also dependent on it. Our future is closely related to our ancient thoughts, ideals, faith and myths.

The authors contends that many aspects of Indian philosophy have much to contribute to the strengthening of the foundations which should provided to the younger generation.

In the present book an attempt has been made to acquint the readers with the wisdom of the great educator's, educational thoughts and educational implications of the sacred literatures. The book aims to provide various perspectives and thoughts of education to the readers.

This book has been mainly designed to serve the requirements of the students of graduate, master and research levels.

In preparation of this book the authors had to refer to the works of other authors and information sources. The authors feels a deep sense of gratitude for incorporating their ideas in the text.

The authors extremely indebted to various authors, editors, educationists, technologists, research scholars, whose views and opinions have been incorporated in this book. The authors grateful to their colleagues, friends, family members and students whose offered suggestions, guidance and assistance. The authors also wish to express thanks to M/s. Infratec Computer Systems, Calicut University for the computerization of the great work.

Finally, the authors whole heartedly expresses their indebtedness to M/s. Kanishka Publishers, Distributors, New Delhi for the meticulous process and publishing of the work. Moreover, all the suggestions and comments are invited for the further improvement of the work.

Dr. S. SABU
ISMAIL THAMARASSERI

Contents

1

Value Education

Introduction

Education is becoming day by day more or less materialistic and the old value traditions are being slowly given up. Today there is an undue emphasis on knowledge-oriented education; which pays attention to the intellectual development of the pupils. This makes the education process one sided. The moral, religious and spiritual values of the great Indian tradition are being pushed back into the wilderness of oblivion consequently in the modern man there is no harmony between the outer life of action and the inner life of saints-emotions. Ancient India was a land of sages and saints-Indians of those days live a value oriented life-religion dominated in their life. Religion was a way of life. But the foreign influence made impure their life. Values have been thrown overboard.

Meaning of Values

A value may be defined in terms of having worth or of being valuable. In this sense we can say that goodness and beauty are values where as evil and ugliness would be disvalues. According to R.K. Mukerjee, "Values are socially approved drives and goals that are internalized through the process of conditioning, learning or socialization and that becomes subjective preferences, standards and aspirations."

Traditional Indian Values

(a) Spiritualism

The ultimate goal of ancient India was other worldly. It was the realization of self or *moksha*. Spirituality means devotion to the spirit, soul, religion or God. It is opposed to materialism and worldliness. It was the ultimate identification of the individual self with the absolute.

(b) Simplicity

Indian saints and seers were embodiments of simplicity and humanity. Gandhiji believed in "simple living and high thinking."

(c) Tolerance

Another characteristic value of ancient time was tolerance. All people were considered to be equal irrespective of caste, creed, vocation etc. Hinduism is the most tolerant of all the religious in the world. Tolerance is the essence of vedic culture.

(d) Dignity of Labour

Labour and hardwork were never treated and never looked down. From royal people to common people every one was engaged in one kind of activity or the other working for the sake of the society.

(e) Self-realization

Self-realization was another important value upheld by the ancient Indians. There is only one supreme reality i.e., God. There is a divine spirit in every human being. Man has to realize the divine presence in him. This realization is known as self-realization.

Value Education in the Present India

The mind set that education is "valueless" has persisted all through these decades and more with India earning the dubious as harbouring the largest number of the poor infrastructure in education.

By value education we refer to planned educational action aimed at the development of proper attitudes, values, emotions and character in the learners. This covers all aspects of personality development-intellectual, social, moral, aesthetic and spiritual. Dimensions of value education should integrate with and enrich the entire curriculum. A more comprehensive understanding of value education would involve critical consideration of several aspects- the general relation between society and values, the objectives and scope of a programme of value education, the sources, methods and strategies of value development and role of teacher as a value education.

The Scope of Value Education

The score of value education in formal learning institutions is determined by the extent, quality and intensity of school influences in relation to the out-of-school influences especially, the media, the peers, home and country. The major objectives of value education in schools are to awaken in the students the appropriate moral aesthetic and cultural sensibilities, enhance their ability to effect with an open mind on moral issues and to develop concern for and commitment to live by the values. The specific values which schools should transmit derive from universalistic perceptions and also from contemporary social and national concerns. Examples for this values and value concerns are democracy, social justice, social cohesion and national unity, scientific temper, secularism, population and quality of life and peace. In keeping with comprehensive nature value education involves adoption of a wide range of methods and strategies as are appropriate to develop knowledge, educate feelings and emotions and train will and character of the learners.

Need for Value Education

Gandhiji considers values as an inseparable component in the full flowering and development of personality. For him every value component is a typical way of life that distinguished one human being from another.

These values are also considered as determinants of human behaviour. They play vital role in the lives of every individual. Values are enduring, and they facilitate standards that guide the conduct of human beings.

We are constantly being reminded that there has been a substantial erosion of values, the fabric of society is being from and age-old ties are breaking up value education aims to provide direction for personal, emotional, social, cultural, moral and spiritual development.

Value Education is a Process of Education

It is essentially a process of working on one's outlooks, beliefs and perception with a view to develop capacities of effective thinking and independent judgement on issues that are of critical concern to oneself and to humanity.

Value Education is a Comprehensive Process

It involves working on the total personality of the individual keeping in view all aspects of personality development, the intellectual, social and emotional will and character. It involves developing sensitivity to and awareness of what is eight, what is good, what is beautiful, ability to choose the right value in accordance with one's conception of the highest ideas of life and internationalizing and realizing them in through and action.

Although all education by definition is a kind of value education, deliberate trust on value education has become necessary in view of the crisis in values which the society is passing through. It refers to a programme of planned educational action aimed at the development of values and character. It is a process of education and being so focuses on the development of critical thinking, rational choice and action respecting the autonomy of the learner. It is not authoritarian indoctrination of dogmas or imposition of do's and don't. It involves development of awareness of the sensitivity to moral and aesthetic phenomena, education of the emotions and training of will and character, i.e., it is concerned with the development of the total person.

Classification of Values

It depends upon the dominant desire in man. Dominant means clearly visible, persistent, positive and socially prized. Anything which gives greater pleasure, greater respect and greater enjoyment, we say that thing has higher value in it.

1. *Higher and Lower Values*

The classification of values into higher and lower is recognized by all schools of philosophy except Indian materialists and their counterparts elsewhere.

2. *Permanent Values and Temporary Values*

Classification of values can also be done on the basis of reality. Materialists view that the main objective of life is enjoying pleasure and wealth. They disagree with the spiritualists that morality and emancipation are of permanent nature. Spiritualists view that the entire creation possesses a higher value because it is created by the supreme. Materialists view that the creation becomes valuable because the man is giving importance to it. He is giving the value to it. At any time, if the thing serves the purpose, the value becomes utilitarian value too.

3. *Intrinsic and Instrumental Values*

There is another classification of values into intrinsic and instrumental ones. If a value helps in the achievement of certain end, it is said to be instrumental. Instrumental values are subjective. If a boy is studying the subject for the sake of knowledge it becomes intrinsic. Thus, same subject is becoming intrinsic and instrumental depending upon the use of it. Intrinsic values and instrumental values are relative in their nature.

4. *Indian Philosophy-Classification of Values*

Indian philosophy believes in four values called "purusharthas", viz., *Dharma, Artha, Kama* and *Moksha*. *Dharma* is ethics, *Artha* is wealth, *Kama* is pleasure and *Moksha* is liberation.

Dharma and *Moksha* were viewed as higher and supreme values where *Artha* and *Kama* are viewed as lower values. *Artha* and *Dharma* are held as instrumental values, *Kama* and *Moksha* are considered as permanent or absolute values and *Artha* and *Kama* as temporary values. The highest value is the highest reality and the lowest value is the lowest reality.

5. *Values Based on Motivation*

Based on motivation also values could be classified into two categories: *Egoism* and *Altruism*. Egoists think that one's actions should serve one's own self-interests. Egoism is generally equated with selfishness.

Altruism opposes egoism. Here in it the individual realizes his fullest selfhood, but this is done is pursuit of the interests of others. Altruism is considered as higher value compared to Egoism.

6. *Aesthetics*

Aesthetics falls into the category of experiences. Aesthetics discusses about the creation of beautiful things. Naturalists believe the experiences are purely natural. All natural things are higher values and all artificial things are lower values.

Idealists believe art is the flower of life. Music is the highest form of art. Realists assert that there is a close connection between refinement of one's perception and the ability to experience and enjoy values.

Pragmatists hold all the experiences are of changing nature, not static. Whichever experience generates greater happiness to greater number of people, becomes an experience of a higher value.

7. *Religious Values*

Naturalism believes that the value raising force is the nature. Any religion which gives supreme importance to the nature is the real religion. Idealism believes that religious values are real. They are of a higher value. Pragmatists hold that values occur through social interaction. Social interaction leads to social experience. Since the society is constantly changing, the values also get changed.

8. *Social Values*

Naturalism believes that the society depends on natural order. Social values are synthetic and bind individuals together. Idealism believes that the spiritualism is a higher value for the individual and society. Realism believes that all physical experiences which do not injure the legal and justified interests of others are considered to be higher in nature. Pragmatists believe that individual and society both are equally important. Almost all values are achieved through the life process of individual and society.

Besides the above classification, values can also be classified as: *(a)* Ethical, *(b)* Organic, *(c)* Recreational, *(d)* Economic, *(e)* Political, *(f)* Personal and *(g)* Intellectual.

(a) Ethical Values

These are moral goods in nature. These are of two kinds: immediate and ultimate. Some give importance to immediate good and some others give importance to the ultimate good.

(b) Organic Values

These arise out of man's desire for self-sustenance, self-preservation which includes food, clothing, health, strength and sex. Those are also called basic values or primary values.

(c) Recreational Values

The desire of the human being and his involvement in different kinds of play and recreation are known as values of pleasure.

(d) Economic Values

All subjects that have an exchange value may be said to be economic values.

(e) Political Values

These values arise out of the man's desire for power.

(f) Personal Values

These are the values which a person cherishes as his own.

Conclusion

The value education programme would require greater professional competence on the part of teachers to mould the thought and behaviour of youths as cherished in our constitution. Therefore the strategy of value education is formed carefully. This value education can play an important role in the present Indian context. A vigourous programme of value education is the need of the hour.

REFERENCES

1. A. Antony—*Teacher and Education in Indian Society.*
2. C. Seshadri, M.A. Khader & G.L. Ahuja—*Education in Values.*
3. J.C. Aggarwal—*Teacher and Education in a Developing Society.*
4. K. Sivarajan—*Trends and Developments in Modern Educational Practice.*
5. N.L. Gupta—*Value Education—Theory and Practice.*

2

Significance of Value Education in the Present Indian Context

India is the country of values, morals and cultures for centuries. Let whatever happens around the world, we can never give up our basic treasures. With standard education systems, good role models in caring parents, dedicated teachers, national heroes and responsible government and society, India's children grew up as *intellectual 'human beings'* for over the years, with the pure understanding of values. Each era gave them role models and they followed them with much enthusiasm. Before independence of India, their role models were Mahatma Gandhi, Bhagat Singh and other freedom fighters. During the freedom struggle, it was the dream of every youngster to be a freedom fighter and every school in the country was the training ground for freedom fighting. In the independent India, we still got some role models in Mother Theresa like persons.

Unfortunately, the system started changing for quite some time. The society's icon of the role model has changed to a rich man. The mentality of people have changed to such a way, that the richness is the measurement for a good life. Each and every person is aspiring to become rich, as much as possible and as quickly as possible at any cost. And the process of getting rich instantly is at the cost of values.

Education is important and imperative for a successful working force for our future. It prepares us with the necessary knowledge that is required to become a doctor or lawyer or civil servant. Now a days we see doctors who take away the kidneys of their patients without even telling them; brilliant engineers and contractors, whose creations collapse as soon as their bills are passed; dignified civil servants who turn to unquestioned emperors; politicians with bag full of false promises.... list continues. Perhaps all of them have received the best education from the best institutions. But that just become a tool for personal prosperity even at the cost of others happiness. The common Indian has become selfish and self-centered. Media has played an important role in changing attitudes of society. And it is a shocking news that the generations of today and the future is growing to this mentality of selfishness, without caring for even the basic human values.

Here arouse the need of value education, for the future of India, for the future of India's children.

Values, What?

Today everybody talks of value education, value based politics and value based society. All of us feel that the values are diminishing and we blame others for not caring for it, while we ourselves are responsible for this situation. But what are these values? They are a set of desirable behaviour, which is good for the individual and also the society which includes caring, courage, fairness, honesty, initiative, perseverance, respect, responsibility, team work, trust worthiness, etc. Value education refers to a wide range of learning and activities of appropriate social behaviour, heritage, democracy, social equality and secularism, physical and mental health and hygiene, etiquette and manners, equality of the sexes, protection of the environment, removal of social barriers, civic rights and duties to aesthetic and even religious training.

Concepts of Value Education

Value education cannot be done through preaching, sermonizing and pontificating, but it is best imparted through process itself. Value education is developing appropriate behaviour and habits. The ability to make moral judgement based on sound reasoning is a very important aim of value education. It is the 'training of the heart' and consists in developing the right feelings and emotions. A moral person is not only a person who does the 'right' thing but also one who does the 'right' thing for the 'right' reason.

The subject value education has been projected as one of national priority in the National Educational Policy (NPE), 1986. The policy declares: "the growing concern over the erosion of essential values and an increasing cynicism in society has brought to focus the need for readjustments in the curriculum in order to make education a forceful tool for the cultivation of social and moral values'. The crisis of values our society is passing through "demands more explicit and deliberate educational efforts towards value development."

Objectives of Value Education

Traditional objectives of value education were based on religion and philosophy. In the modern world the objectives changed. A civilized individual must posses certain minimum social skills. Value education should prepare an individual to meet these demands.

The major dimensions on value education are physical education, emotional education, mental development, aesthetic development and the moral and spiritual domain. The values to be pursued in the moral and spiritual realm, are: sincerity, faithfulness, obedience, gratitude, honesty, benevolence, generosity, cheerfulness, selflessness, freedom from egoism, self control in joy and suffering, in honour and dishonour, success and failure, pursuit of the deepest and the highest of the absolute and ultimate and the progressive expression of this pursuit in thought, feeling and action.

The objectives of value education should be such that the curriculum should enable the pupils to employ modern skills for the betterment of mankind while helping them renew their commitment to fundamental traditional values.

In our secular country the government should consider the contribution of religious in developing an effective value education programme can be developed without relying on religion. At the same time, common teachings of all religions can be used to reinforce values and also teach religious tolerance and understanding to children. An important aspect of value education programmes in all countries relates to the development of the spirit of national identity and patriotism in children. This is necessary for the purpose of integrating and strengthening a nation. An important objective of value education should be to make children aware of the fact that the whole world is now a community of interdependent nations that the survival and well being of the people of the world depends on mutual co-operation. Value Education objectives must make them able to think right, to feel the right kind of emotions and to act in the desirable manner.

Role of Teachers and Parents in Imparting Values

Two categories of people who make maximum impact on the personality of an individual in the formative years of life, which remains all through the life, are the parents and the teachers. It is this class of people who become role models-good or bad, without their consent or knowledge.

Role of Parents

House is the first learning environment for the child and parents are the first teachers. They not only guide the child in its progressive path but also demonstrate the appropriate behaviour by their actions. Only an 'iron hand in a velvet glove' can provide the necessary firm guidance without being unduly harsh. The impressions that the child gets in the initial part of his life, remains with him. What a person becomes when he grows up is very largely determined by the unbringing. Parent's action is more important than their saying. And they have no options but to become role models.

Role of Teachers

Teacher is a source of information, a guide, a mentor, a substitute parent, a motivator all at the same time. Teaching is the only profession which always deals with the future. The ideal teacher should be a lover of subject, profession and the students. According to Confucius only a person who is always a source of love, morally upright and whose behaviour not only in personal but also in the institutional life is fault less is worthy of being a teacher.

Even though the position of teacher has moved from the sole source of information to among many, they still are most important key factor in education system. The society is becoming more materialistic and values appear to be pushed into the background. Value education should be undertaken as an integral part of teaching of all courses by all teachers and through a systematized pattern of life.

Role of Government

By undertaking the need for value education, the government has taken many steps in the education system of the country. NCERT, being the apex organization in the area of school education, has been identified as the National Resource Centre for value education by the government, with a view to promoting value orientation of school education at all levels. A core group on value education has been formed for the centre with the functions to develop and execute plans, programmes and activities for value orientation of school education and provide the resources and materials.

Content and Learning Methods

Social and ethical values; examples from day-to-day situations; saying and biographies of great men; dramas, dialogues, stories from religion and mythology, simple poems, proverbs and scriptures from world religions, yoga and other activities that develop self-discipline; group activities like cleaning the school campus, visiting slums, visits to hospitals and places of worship of different faiths; discussions on values like self sacrifice, collective happiness, love for truth and ultimate values of life-love, beauty, goodness-'Personality Development Retreats' to develop self-control, punctuality, sharing and caring respect for other faiths, co-operation and the value of silence; develop the quality of 'dignity' of labour'; celebrating special days etc. can be practiced in value education system.

Value education cannot be forced on children through text books and examination. Teachers and parents need to be motivated, inspired and consistent in their words and deeds. They must radiate the values they want the children to learn. It is important to alter the every day rhythm of schooling; it must encourage the spirit of co-operation, togetherness and creativity.

Our country would awaken once again to those eternal values for which it has stood for many centuries. Only an ideal teacher, ideal parent and ideal government who themselves are the inspirational light of values can lead a society in the right direction. They have to demonstrate the essential values such as optimism, motivation, willingness to learn and teach, truth, non-violence, never to speak and think ill of others, creativity and ability to demonstrate love. That is the responsibility that the society must take in order to be an effective catalyst for social change.

REFERENCES

1. *Deepika Education*—Supplement, October 2003.
2. Joan S. *et al.*, (Ed.)—*Values in Education.*
3. Narayan—*Man, Education and Values*. Delhi: B.R. Publishing Corporation.

3

Human Rights Education

What Are Human Rights?

Human Rights, the most fundamental of all rights, are the rights of people have simply because they are people. These rights belongs to each person; man, women and child. They are the right to life, liberty including all political, civil, social, economic, cultural rights necessary for people to live dignified lives. They are the unalienable birth rights of all members of human family. They are to be enjoyed by all without discrimination with regard to race, gender, language, religion, political, social or national origin, property birth or other status.

The underlying principles of the global human rights struggle include the following; Recognition of the equity and dignity of all individuals, recognition of cultural diversity as a fundamental human value, recognition and guarantee of the fundamental equality of all persons in human rights without discrimination with regard to race, creed, colour, nationality, ancestry, language, gender, place of origin or other status.

As the universal declaration of Human Rights says "all members of the human family are created free and equal in dignity."

Human Rights: Classification

1. *Fundamental Freedom*: These are the rights to freedom of speech, religion and assembly.
2. *Legal Rights*: These are the rights to freedom from arbitrary arrest, unreasonable search or seizure of property, arbitrary imprisonment, self-incrimination and unfair adjudication.

3. *Equalitarian Rights*: These are the rights to equality and to access to employment, education, housing and service without discrimination on the basis of race, religion, sex or the other irrelevant characteristics.
4. *Economic Rights*: These are the rights to every one to an adequate standard of living by having adequate food, clothing and housing including the Rights to gain a living by working, the Rights to own property and right to contact with others.

Development of Human Rights

Most of societies have had traditions similar to the 'golden rule' of "do unto others as you would have them do unto you."

Human Rights have been debated and developed throughout history. Signified events that lend to development of human right is sequenced as follows:

AD 1215—The king of England agrees to Magna Carta. King John of England proclaimed and established 2 fundamental principles *(i)* There are certain laws so essential to organization that the sovereign must obey them *(ii)* If the sovereign refuses to obey them, the people have the right to force him to do so or put another government in its place. Thus government must responsible to the will of people.

AD 1675	–	Habeas Corpus Act passed
	–	Magna Carta Official Law
	–	Bill of Rights
1825	–	Slavery abolished in British empire
1850	–	The United States of America abolished slavery by adding 13th Amendment
1900	–	Women allowed the vote in Britain
1945	–	Formation or the United Nations Organizations
1948	–	UN created universal declaration of Human Rights
1959	–	Declaration of Human Rights of the child by the UN
1966	–	The covenant of Economic, Social and Cultural Rights
	–	The covenant on Civil and Political Rights
2000	–	Decade for Human Rights Education (1995-2009).

However the most significant even leading to change and Rapid development in the domain of Human Rights was the second world war. The mass killing of Jews between 1933-45 is unquestionably the grossest violation of Human Right in the modern history. The only crime that had been committed by these people was belonging to a different racial, religion or ethnic group. The resulted shock and horror lead to steps for protection of human rights internationally. In 1945, fifty one countries joined together to form United Nations and pledged to take 'joined action' to protect Human Rights. It was followed by universal declaration of Human Rights by UN General Assembly in 1948 and this was followed by a number of covenant such as Economic, Social, Political, Cultural and Civil Rights of 1966. These all lead to International Bill of Rights; which includes the following documents. The United Nations charter, Universal Declaration of Human Rights. The covenant on civil and political rights, the covenant in economic, social, cultural rights, the optional protocol to the covenant of civil and political rights.

HUMAN RIGHTS AND EDUCATION

Rationale for Human Rights Education

Human Rights are important because they;

1. Protect us from discrimination.
2. Protect us from unfamiliar treatment.
3. Promote the development of democratic values and attitudes and freedom.
4. Provide awareness of society at large and insights into institutional structure and cultural values.

The hightend awareness of human rights and informed world opinion are essential for the protection and implementation of Human Rights. Human Rights are essential part of the social studies curriculum, that will develop global perspectives. Human Right abuses as history reveals, sow the seeds of future wars. Effective Human Rights education is a necessary pre-condition for a healthy democratic society, especially in times of crisis. Human Rights education promoting the positive role of governments, international and non-governmental agencies in mitigating abuses of human rights in the world. Human Rights education promotion responsibilities on citizens in a participatory democracy. It develops global awareness. Developing all human beings as human rights literate.

OBJECTIVES OF HUMAN RIGHTS EDUCATION

Human Rights Education Must Aim At

1. ***Knowledge About Human Rights***

   (a) Developing the concept of Human Rights and other related concepts as they have come to be used to the global context especially in the 20th century.

   (b) Developing and understanding about the Human Rights documents such as universal declaration of Human Rights. The international covenants, the Canadian charter of Rights and freedom.

   (c) Making an awareness of Human Rights institutions and mechanism of protection.

2. ***Values and Attitudes Infavour of Rights of Human***

   (a) To develop a sense of empowerment by asserting that all individuals have the right to be free from arbitrary and unreasonable exercise of authority.

   (b) Developing appreciation and respect for the right of others.

   (c) To develop toleration and other behaviours and attitudes consistent with Human Rights principles.

   (d) To show empathy for those who are denied rights.

   (e) To identify prejudices and discriminations through critical and objective thinking.

   (f) To promote values to seek a high level of social justice, equity and fairness.

   (g) Developing appreciation for essential worth of others and commonality of needs, rights, aspirations, behaviours and talents which bind human kind.

3. ***To Promote Skills in Favour of Human Rights***

   (a) To adopt peaceful solutions which respect Human Rights through mediation and conflict resolution.

   (b) To developing social skills of respecting people of diverse cultural backgrounds through interaction and communication.

   (c) To accepting responsibilities by following that for every right there is a responsibility.

   (d) To practicing democratic decision making process.

   (e) To develop skills to apply Human Rights instruments and institutional mechanism for the protection and implementation of Human Rights.

Ten Principles of Human Rights Education

There are ten principles, which are the anchor sheet on which human right education is based. The principles listed below should be followed in all aspects of human rights education.

1. Provide open-minded examination of Human Rights issues and concerns with ample opportunities for participants to arrive at positions different from those of presenter.
2. Avoid too much focus on Human Rights abuses. Emphasize Human Rights as a positive value system and a standard to which every one is entitled.
3. Include an international/global dimension to the Human Rights topic being discussed-how it manifest it self at home and abroad.
4. Keep in mind that, every issue or topic of human rights with universal declaration of Human Rights. Make the connection explicit.
5. Emphasize on belief that the individual can make a difference and substantiate with examples who have done so in the course of time.
6. Include action dimension that provides participants with opportunities to act on their beliefs and understandings. These actions should address problems both at home and else were around the globe.
7. Be responsive to concerns related to cultural diversity, which includes perspectives such as gender, race, religion and national traditions.
8. Keep lecturing to a minimum. Use participatory methods such as discussion, role playing, debates, games, simulations and case studies.
9. Keep content, learning process and the class environment in mind. So keep the respect for justice and human dignity in the environment in which the session is conducted.
10. Connect people's lived experiences directly to abstract concepts dealt with in human rights education and legal documents.

Setting the Classroom Climate for Human Rights Education

Teaching Human Rights is sensitive and serious matter. It is as much a process as content. It requires student involvement and participation. It should be an open classroom rather than a stifled one. In setting a classroom climate for teaching Human Rights, teachers can help in the following ways.

1. Organize classrooms and classroom strategies so that all students can practice and experience Human Rights behaviours as well as talk about them without hesitation.
2. Involve all students in making a set of classroom rules and responsibilities as an effective way to start teaching for Human Rights.
3. Respect all opinions.
4. Avoid putdowns.
5. Use conflict situations and provide opportunities for talking about Human Rights issues. In essence conflict promotes enquiry.
6. Engage the students in discussing and role playing moral conflict and Human Rights issues.
7. Arrange action oriented activities rather than talk oriented activities for Human Rights teaching. For example discussing and role playing is more effective than seat work.
8. Use more group activities, involve parents and community in a few classroom activities.
9. Seek the support of the principal in setting the classroom climate.

METHODS TO PROMOTE HUMAN RIGHTS THROUGH EDUCATION

There are numerous strategies, methods, techniques and approaches are available to deal with Human Rights in the global context. Methods used in classroom are as follows:

1. 'Brain Storming'

Brainstorming is a strategy to generate ideas and get the full rolling. The major purpose is to stimulate thinking and bringing out a great range of ideas. Students are encouraged to come with up creative, exciting and radical ideas without fear of criticism or evaluation. Divide the classroom into small group consisting 5 to 8 members. Let them select a recorder and chain person. Explain the basic rules of brainstorming. Present the issue to be brainstormed.

Guidelines for Using Brainstorming

1. Identify the problem or issue to be brainstormed and present it in simple language.
2. Write everything down; do not judge or evaluate the ideas.
3. Consider using more than one recorder so idea are lost.
4. Emphasize some basic rules which should be enforced.

Rules of Brainstorming

1. No judgement or evaluation of ideas
2. 'The sky is the limit'
3. The more ideas, the better
4. Piggyback on others ideas
5. Keep the process informed and relaxed
6. Record all ideas
7. Use the brainstorming when a lot of ideas are needed or when the time is limited.

A Sample of Brain Storming on Human Right Teaching

Level : Secondary school students

Time : 45 minutes

Topic : Ways of Studying Human Rights in Global Context

Levels of Thinking : Comprehension to synthesis

Objectives : Students in small groups will be able to give different ways of studying human rights issues in the global context. Students follow rules for brainstorming

Material : Blackboard

Strategy : Topic: In what ways might we learn about the Human Rights in the world today?

Step 1 : Divide the class in small groups. Let them select the chain and recorder. Give the topic explain the grouped rules for brain storming.

Step 2 : Students go to work.

Step 3 : Sample ideas often 30 minutes.

- Examine the Universal Declaration of Human Rights (UDHR).
- Invite a refuge from Somalia, Haiti, Cuba, Bosnia, Sudan or role play as refugee.
- Invite Amnesty international representative.
- Do independent research on Human Rights issue.
- Search the newspapers on Human Rights issues.
- Ask the teacher to provide an overall view of Human Rights in the global context related concepts.
- Discussion on Human Rights and prioritization of Rights and responsibilities.
- Campaigning, action projects for rights.
- Make rights charts, rights displays, rights mistrals, right exhibition, rights bingo, oppression game and rights auction.

Step 4 : Discussion, selection of projects/ideas and other activities to follow.

It is Okay to:

- Say whatever comes to mind
- Have the same idea as others
- Add or slightly change ideas
- Be silent
- Wait for a while.

It is not Okay to:

- Criticize ideas
- Discuss the ideas at this time
- Talk while some one is still speaking.

Comments:

- It is okay to be silent, people need time to think.
- It is okay to wait and have another go at list later.
- It is not okay to make comments that are hurtful.

2. Co-operative Learning Strategy—The Jigsaw Strategy

In the past two decades considerable attention has been given to co-operative learning strategies in teaching learning practice. In this students work together to achieve a particular goal. Five basic elements are required to facilitate the co-operative learning strategy. They include positive interdependence, individual accountability, face to face interaction, interpersonal and social skills and group processing.

The Jigsaw Strategy

The Jigsaw developed by Aronson (1978) is the most powerful co-operative learning strategies used in Social Studies, literature, science and other curriculum areas, where the development of concepts rather than specific skills is objective. A large amount of content can be covered in less time with greater learning retention. A sample of Jigsaw strategy is as follows:

Standard : XIth, XIIth classes.

Level of Thinking : Comprehension to Application.

Objectives : 1. To develop concept of Human Rights and other associated terms.

2. To become familiar with articles in the U.D.H.R.

3. To develop communication skills in small groups and their respective learning objectives.

Materials : Packets of material developed by teachers blackboard.

Strategy :

Step 1 : Objectives are classified. The class is divided into 'home groups'. Then each member is assigned to an expert group.

Step 2 : Expect groups are provided with a special list of materials. They do further research, and add to the list. Students read material together and determine procedures for returning to teach their home group about the material (after they have 'specialized' in it).

Step 3 : Students return to their home groups. Group members take turns presenting their 'specialized material' and their perspective. Participants should check for understanding among home group members.

Step 4 : Students participate in oral evaluation to demonstrate understanding of the material present to the home groups. The teacher helps in processing how well their groups worked and about changes that might be made next time.

3. Socratic Questioning

Socratic questioning or Socratic dialogue is a variation of Socratic method. The role do teacher is that of a guide who questions and helps them to examine and clarify their own views and opinions and develop sound reasoning. It is also teaching by asking questions and thus leading the audience into logical contradiction. The Greek sage Socrates is the model for this type of instruction. Instead of talking at students, the teacher participates in dialogues with them, aiming to uncover the rightness or wrongness of their beliefs.

The Essence of Socratic Method is Capsuled below:

1. Objectives should be clear and techniques should suit the objective.
2. Socrates methods involves a strategy consisting of four parts:
   - *(a)* A student states an initial propositions.
   - *(b)* The teacher leads the student to doubt.
   - *(c)* The teacher gets the student to admit that he does not know the way out of perplexity.
   - *(d)* The teacher guides the student in the persuit of truth about the issue.
3. The Socratic method involves the perplexity serves as the motivation for further enquiry.
4. People clarify the thoughts by testing them against alternatives.
5. Socrates used this method among friends who were adults with a great deal of experiences of the world.
6. The Socratic method could cause tension to and discomfiture of the respondents.
7. Socrates typically used his method for enquiring into moral issues for which there were no correct answers.
8. Many critics do not accept the notion of innate ideas of the Socratic method.
9. It is slow and complicated.

4. The Talking Circle

Students sit in a circle or in a number of smaller circles of 10-15 students rather than in rows facing the teacher. Everyone is provided as opportunity to speak uninterrupted. An object such as a stone or a piece of wood can be passed from students to student to signify that person with the object has the floor.

The talking circle or 'heart sharing' was originally a tradition of Hopi Indian of North America known as the talking stick. Tribal Members gathered in a sacred ceremonial room called 'kiva' for their council meetings. The meeting was structured in such a way that every one would have an opportunity to participate while having full attention of everybody present. A strict rule was followed that a person have a special stick had the floor and was not to be interepted while speaking.

There are various forms of talking circles exists. The members could be vary depending on the size of the class. It is a strategy for providing structured time for students to share their feelings, hopes, concerns and appreciations, to discuss a particular issue or problem.

Rules of Talking Circle

1. Only the person with a special object talks.
2. The object must be passed carefully to next person.
3. It is okay to miss one's turn if one does not feel ready to speak. Just pass the object to the next person. There should be no negative consequences, however subtle, for saying "I Pass."
4. The teacher should ensure that every one must feel invited to participate.
5. Talk about what you feel or think, not about what some else said.
6. Listen carefully, don't use listening time to plan what you are going to speak.
7. Make a promise not to tell any one else what some shared.
8. Every one has 2-3 minutes to share. Be thoughtful. Don't take some one less time, feel free and contribute as much possible.

5. Role Playing

Role playing is a acting out of a situation or a problem. It is a way of exploring a problem together as a class. It provides the opportunities for testing ideas and plans of action in a practice situation. Through role playing the students get to experience how it feels to do something rather than just talk about it. Role playing the actual acting out of feeling and behaviours. Students take on a role and act out feelings and behaviours of act out about they think the 'roles' behaviours and feelings would be given specified circumstances. Through role paying students can learn new information, analyze alternatives, identify and examine feelings and gain social skills in work in groups.

The major purpose of role playing is to get the student into another identity, providing opportunities to perceive how others might feel, think, or act. Many role plays set students upto experience stressful, unfamiliar or controversial situation. The general purpose of role playing is to feel different perceptions and perspectives.

There are four steps in the role play:

1. Setting a Scene
   The task in this step is to provide the reason for the role and to prepare the group. Several strategies can be used to set the stage. Those strategies include; discussion to raise issues, a lecture to provide a focus, a case study to outline the situation.
2. The Role Play
   The following points compraise this step;
   - The teacher assigns roles or calls for volunteers.
   - Outlines the roles to player in a concised manner.
   - Players should given a short time to discuss together on the roles they have assigned.
   - Those not involved in role playing act as observers. Observers are given instructions to observe what and how to look on the play.

Begin the Role Play

Let it run until the point is made.

Let it the teacher could decide how much time should be given. The following steps are to be counted for this.

(i) By asking players to change roles in 'Vs' rs them situation.
(ii) Interrupt the role play and conduct a brief interview with key players. Inquire about how things are going, make suggestions.

(iii) After a few minutes of Role playing stop the action and ask for a demonstration of particular skill. For instance, in court scenes, the players could be asked for an example of 'objection'.

3. Debriefing
The players could be asked to respond on their feelings. It is important that this is done before observers are given the opportunities to respond to role play.

- Players could be moved out of their roles sometimes physical movement is necessary.
- The observers are asked to report what they observed and learned. Descriptions of actual behaviours rather than interpretations should be emphasized.

4. Closure
Summarized what they learned. Link the role play back to the material previously discussed.

REFERENCES

1. Agarwal (1983). *Implementation of Human Rights Covenants with Special Reference to India.* Allahabad: Kitab Mahal.
2. Batra, T.S. (1979). *Human Rights – A Critique.* New Delhi: Metropolitan Book Co., (P) Ltd.
3. Baxi, Upendra. (Ed.) (1987). *The Right to be Human.* New Delhi: Lancer International.
4. Chand, Attar. (1985). Politics of Human Rights and Civil Liberties. Delhi: UDH Publishers.
5. Graves, N. (1990). *Teaching for International Understanding, Peace and Human Rights.* Paris: UNESCO.
6. Tarrow (Ed.) (1989). *Human Rights and Education* (2nd Ed.). New Jersey: Douglass Coll.
7. Vandenberg (1990). *Education as Human Rights: A Theory of Curriculum and Pedagogy.* New Delhi: Teacher's College Press.

4

Freedom in Education

The Quest for Freedom

Most of the critical issues of life cluster about man's quest for freedom-freedom from the bondage of ignorance and freedom from the bondage of precedent and custom.

In this day man's restless search for freedom from bondage of ignorance and the precedent had precipitated a social crisis. He has been largely freed from the old insecurities that arose from his very limited power to predict and control the activities of row nature. But he has run himself into new insecurities that come from the artificial social and economic systems which his enlarged power over natural energies have led him to devise. Freedom from these new insecurities is of a piece with his freedom from the old; it lies in the direction of a more effective use of science and the scientific method in regulating this artificial systems of his own creation. Right and Wrong, this derive their meaning in terms of harmony or disharmony with the universe and the only freedom that man can ever hope to enjoy is the "freedom to do right."

Freedom is the progressive disappearance of all restrictions on the unfolding of potentialities of individuals, as human beings and not as a logs in the wheel of the mechanical social organism. Man's freedom is the highest moral standard according to the human ethics.

The word freedom is used in different contents. Originally it comes from the word 'free' and is a condition for living. Freedom is the birth right of all human being. Man is bornfree. No body likes inferences. The dictionary meaning of the word freedom is 'independence'. It can also be personal liberty. Freedom is only an idea which exist only in certain facts. The term freedom can be viewed from three senses;

1. Freedom from restraints
2. Freedom of choosing
3. Religious sense.

1. *Freedom from Restraints*

Freedom is the first and basic sense means freedoms from restraints or restrictions. It also implies salvation which denies laws and conventions, fears and restraints. Obviously freedom leads to happiness which comes from within. It is assumed that freedom is good itself. Freedom is a compount area which stands for a number of conditions and states of mind. These constraints may be external or internal. External constraints may be political, social, religious, cultural, moral etc. and internal constraints may be personnel or psychological.

2. *Freedom of Choosing*

This is the traditional freedom of the will. A man is said to be free to extent that he can choose his own goals or course of conduct and can choose between alternative available to him and is not compelled to act as he would not him self choose to act or prevented from acting.

3. *Religious Sense*

In this sense, freedom is the freedom or liberty to choose and accept the will of the god. This is only the spiritual freedom. Thus every one has the right to acquire the will of the God.

Freedom

Freedom is a word used in various contexts. It has different connotations. It is a condition of human living, a particular state of mind but it is not a licence. It is a concept which is opposite to the concept of bondage.

It is sometimes used in negative sense. Yet it may be positive. It refers to certain values. Freedom in the first and basic sense means freedom from restraints and all kind of constraints. It also implies salvation which demices laws and conventions, fears and restraints.

Even freedom ignores impulse inhibition. It is wonderful to have freedom which is enhanced by values. Freedom leads to happiness which comes from within. It is believed that complete detachment is the condition for freedom. In 'Gita' it has been stated that the person who has the capacity to control his impulses has the potential to enjoy freedom. In other words, without freedom, happiness cannot be won. This particular issue of freedom is rather coupler. The questions of fact are mainly two;

What are we free form?
What are we limited by?

The more interesting question of value is what do we want to be free from and why? In short, the question of freedom revolves round the concept of values. It is assumed that freedom is good itself. It is also true that freedom in its prime sense is neither good nor bad. It is a neutral fact. Thus freedom is a compound idea which stands for a number of conditions and states of mind. It is neither good nor bad, but factual. The significance of freedom lies in its use. It can be external or internal. The primary notion of freedom from restraints has a reference to the ethics. The traditional concepts of freedom of will and freedom of choice are some what interrelated.

The ideas of freedom and determination may be examined by the two questions.

Are we free to choose?
To what extent are we free to do so?

Freedom to do this or that, to do or not to do is of great moral importance. If we are not free the question of morality does not arise? It is a fact that freedom is a condition for discipline?

We are free to choose or not to choose within certain limits. We blame mankind for its inconsistency but we are to remember that there is a destiny or fate which play vital roles in our life.

The question of freedom is thus related to other issues. Human beings have been endowed with reasoning which helps him to distinguish the right from the wrong, the good from the bad. It is a power, a capacity to judge the values for the right choice. Freedom is not the same as liberty. We have our own limits and limitations. Freedom from external and internal restrictions and freedom of the will are not the same as liberty. Another dimension of freedom emerges as a result of the exercise of the freedom when in conflict. This can be discovered not only in moral living but through the acceptance of the discipline of learning.

To attain freedom is a supreme end of education. Freedom of a child is the first word of child-centered education. Without freedom personality cannot grow spontaneously. Kant held that all moral acts are not free acts.

"Freedom is the truth of necessity" says Hegal. It is a complains with a law, which is in conformity with our highest nature. According to Kant, in moral action the individual is obeying a law coming from itself. The transcendental freedom of Kant is not accepted by Herbert. Education would be a tyranny if it did not lead to freedom. Freedom may be used as freedom from external strain or freedom of will or choosing freedom from conformity to order, According to professor Reid; freedom is mental detachment. Dewey mentions, positive freedom which involves social guidance.

Determinism and Freedom

The problem of free will, i.e., whether the human will is free to act and not to act or whether it is determined is among the oldest of moral questions. The moralists and guardians of law pleaded in favour of free will. But the behavioural scientists held that free will is impossible due to compelling scientific reasons. The interest in the problem is motivated by the fact that belief in free will is inconsistent with scientific principles and deniel of free will jeopardizes morality and jurisprudence. Thus these are clearly two schools of thought, one holding that all our actions are determined and the other that human will be free in making choices between alternative actions, otherwise the concepts of moral responsibility would be meaningless.

Freedom as the freedom of doing and not doing an act. But the problem arises when it is uncritically accepted that man has the power of free choice, obligation, law guilte and remorse, praise and blame etc. Kant says only 'good will' is free. Good will is nothing but the rational attitude of doing or not doing an act.

The problem of free will is felt to be an urgent problem by an ordinary educated man because it is closely connected with the concept of moral responsibility. We regard a man morally responsible for an act since he is presumed to be free in doing that act. Free will in some sense is an precondition of moral responsibility. The concept of free will is not contrary to scientific belief. The religious conception of sin, atonement, repentance reward become meaningless of freedom of choice between good and bad is taken a man. Freedom is a matter of immediate awareness. The concept of freedom will is incompatible with the view that every action as a cause. No conduct is ever uncaused and ever free.

The concept of reward and punishment also presuppose and freedom of will. The problem of moral freedom is inseparably associated with the ideas of duty. Those who believe in god cannot accept man as the master of his own destiny. Man cannot be endowed with the power to choose between good and evil, when we accept God as sole determining force.

With the emergence of science in the modern age as the chief source of knowledge about nature. The problem of free will was viewed from scientific angle. Science believes the determinism a belief in trees will is unscientific.

A man is free when his conduct is under his own control. He acts under compulsion when some one controls his conduct. Moral responsibility for an act implies freedom and freedom implies self determination.

The Historical Perspective of Freedom

In the history of philosophical and social thought 'freedom' has a specific use as a moral and a social concept to refer either to circumstances which arise in the relations of man to man or to specific conditions of social life. Even when so restricted, important differences of usage are possible and most the political or philosophical argument about the meaning or the nature of freedom is concerned with the legitimacy or convenience of particular applications of the term.

Freedom, from the middle English freedom (the state of being free) the quality of not being constrained by fate, necessity or circumstance in one's decisions and actions.

Absence of Constraint of Coercion

According to European individualism and liberalism, freedom refers primarily to a condition characterized by the absence of coercion or constraint imposed by another person a man is said to be free to the extent that he can choose his own goals or course conduct, can choose between alternatives available to him and it is not compelled to act as he would not himself choose to act, or prevented from acting he us he would otherwise choose to act, by the will of another man, of the state, or of any other authority. Bertrand Russel; "Freedom in general may be defined as the absence of obstacles to the realization of desires."

Kinds of Freedom

When men speak of their being free or claim freedom for themselves, they are referring not only to the absence of coercion and restraint imposed by others (freedom from) but also to that on behalf of which freedom is being claimed (what they are claimed freedom for). This another sense in which we can speak about a positive aspect of freedom.

In political and social discussion, a claim to freedom is almost invariably (albeit usually implicity) a claim to a particular liberty, a claim to freedom for or in the exercise of some particular interest or form of activity.

Thus freedom in the abstract is a class comprising many species.

- Freedom of thought and speech.
- Freedom of worship.
- Freedom of movement.
- Freedom in the use or disposal of ones property.
- Freedom in the choice of ones employer or occupation.
- Freedom from want and fear.
- Freedom from economic in security.

Freedom and Power

Connection between freedom and power when there is conflict between individuals and groups for possession or control of scarce means and conditions of action, control over means is a condition of the availability of alternatives and hence of choice and freedom.

Obviously this relation between inequality of power and inequality of freedom provides one of the connections the exist between liberty and democracy.

FREEDOM AND DISCIPLINE

Freedom can be discussed in various contexts, political, economic, social or educational. Smith, in 'The Democratic Way of Life' defines liberty; "To do as one pleases, this alone is liberty." Harper's definition is, "Freedom is the condition of where the person may do whatever he desires, according to his wisdom and his conscience." Von Hayek's interpretation is more modest; 'Freedom is a condition of men in which the coersion of some by others is reduced as much as possible'.

From the point of view of educational philosophy and practice, is a function of individuality. Brubacher's opinion is that if pupils have no individual differences, there would be no demand for freedom. Every one would act alike, no one would want to be different, or free. Children, we see around us are so different from one another in many ways and yet in many ways they are also alike. Thus any system of education will have to deal with heterogeneity as well as homogeneity. The relation between training in freedom and achievement of self-control is very complex and needs appraisal.

Freedom and discipline are interdependent. Nunn says that discipline is not external, it touches the in most springs of conduct. It controls and vibrates all our emotions and thoughts and gives perfect shape to all our activities. Freedom and discipline are not opposed each other. Bertrand Russell says, "True discipline is not externally controlled but it is spontaneous and it leads to perfect development." John Dewey is also of the opinion that discipline brings social control.

In short, freedom and discipline are two sides of the same coin. Freedom could not be used properly without discipline and discipline cannot be enforced without certain degree of freedom.

Discipline according to Herbert; is a continuous process which resorts to punishment. Freedom in a condition for effective discipline and discipline is the product of freedom. On a critical analysis we find that discipline can be considered as a concept in the sense of control. It may mean self discipline which is involved in exercising one's freedom and joy. One must be reasonably free from external restraint for maintaining the discipline without any imposition.

Discipline is connected with disciples, with pupils, with learning. The art of discipline is the art of making disciples. The word 'discipline' acquires two meanings:

(*a*) Restrictive treatment by teachers and,
(*b*) Order among pupils achieved by this kind of treatment.

According to comprehensive dictionary meaning, discipline is an orderly action by instructing, them in the same way. Another meaning of the word is orderly conduct and action which results from training. Discipline and freedom grow together. They are mutually interdependent. There are two kinds of discipline.

1. Positive
2. Negative

One refers to generation of best human impulses and their application. Discipline is thus a state of mind but order is a state of affairs.

VIEWS ON DISCIPLINE AND FREEDOM

1. The Traditional or Authoritarian School

These thinkers are called 'repressionists' by some and they support the notion that the child should learn unquestioning obedience to the authority of the teacher and parent. The child, according them, is immature, therefore, he does not know as much as the adult. He therefore, needs to have an implicit trust in the authority of the teacher and the parent.

There is three characteristics of the authoritarian method; first, little or no attempt is made to explain to the child or adolescent, the reason for the rules he is expected to submit to; second, it is assumed that his breaking of rules is intentional and he is not given an opportunity to explain his reason for doing so; and third, punishment is almost always corporal and of a harsh and sometimes cruel nature. The authoritarian parent or teacher regards punishment as a reinforcer, consequently the harsher it is, the better it will teach the individual that he must conform to adult commands.

Authoritarian parents and teacher use one of two different types of control; they either use threats that leave the youth in secure and afraid to engage in any new behaviour or they set certain limits, at the same time encouraging the adolescent to engage in approved forms of activity. The second type of control produces better results.

Limitations of the Traditional Method

Childrens are unprepared to meet any future problems that may arise. They lack confidence in their ability to make decisions and to carry them out successfully. Children become submissive if he does not act in an openly rebellious manner. Childrens disliked by members of his peer group because of his arrogant attitude. Over strictness leads to feelings that the world is hostile, causes the young person to reject authority and to assert his independence. Many adolescents drop out of school or leave home when the authoritarian attitude of teachers or parents becomes unreasonable and unbearable.

2. The Emanicipationists or Progressive Educators

They adopt a 'laissez faire' attitude towards children. They consider individual differences among children as fixed features, they defined the freedom of a young to assert the unique differences which characteristic his individuality.

Rousseau, Montessori, A.S. Neill advocate this freedom in education. Rousseau's plea is 'freedom' and 'absence of restraint' for Emile. The doctrine of liberty or freedom and the principle of individuality reflect the emancipationists views of Montessori. A.S. Neill believes that discipline dogmatically imposed and punishments create fear and fear arouses hostility.

3. The Impressionist School

In between the repressionists and the emancipationists there are educators who may be described as 'impressionists'. They are against punishment and traditional repression, and they believe that desirable modes of behaviour in children can be brought about through the teachers personality and personal influence. The teacher has in mind certain standards of behaviour which he tries to establish, not by appealing to fear, but by appealing to the submissive and initiative tendencies in the child. It is a kind of gentle force.

4. Democratic Control

Family relationships and teacher-pupil relations under this from exist when rules are explained and warnings are given about the consequences of breaking rules. There is a training in self-control brought about. External control becomes internal control and the pupil develops a super-ego because he becomes a conscious agent in the process of socialization. The individual achieves the super ego as he links and passes on from the impulsive stage to the problem-solving stage, which has many alternatives to choose from and he makes his own choice.

ESSENTIALS OF DISCIPLINE

1. Education in Moral Concepts

Parents and teachers assume that when a child grown-up, he has learnt what is right or wrong, and that no further training is needed. This is incorrect. As the child becomes an adolescent, his social horizons widen and boys as well as girls should realize what boundaries society places on them. They should know what actions society will tolerate under any new situations. Rules and laws have the function of teaching the individual what these boundaries are, so that he may act in a desirable manner.

2. Reward for Socially Approved Behaviour

There are two purposes of giving rewards; firstly, rewards have an educational value, they tell the adolescent that his behaviour is socially approved and therefore it is 'good' behaviour. Secondly, they are ego supporting and this stimulates and encourages him, so that he can continue to act in that way.

3. Punishment for Intentional Wrong Doing

It deters the repetition of socially undesirable acts and it shows the adolescent what the social group considers wrong. Punishment can be physical or corporal or it can be form of detention, extra assignments, isolation, humiliation, suspension from school, academic failure etc. From the philosophical point of view, punishment has been justified on the basis of the retribution or realization theory. According to this theory, punishment is a sort of revenge. Again, some justify punishment on the grounds that it protects society by making an example of the offender, in other words. It acts as a deterrent. In the classroom, anti-social behaviour is punished in order to protect other students.

A third theory of punishment which justified its use or non use, is called educative. According to this theory, only that punishment should be administered which can re-educate the offender. The offender, through the punishment, realizes what he has done, how others see his offence and how he can improve his behaviour. If punishment is to serve the purpose of aiding in self control and in being educative, it should have the following characteristics.

1. It should be related in some form to the misbehaviour.
2. It should be certain and consistent.
3. It must be fair and just.
4. It should be impersonal.
5. It should be constructive and conductive to better self-control.
6. Punishment should be withheld until the child's motive for the offence is understood.
7. The punishment should not arouse fear in the childs mind.
8. It should not involve the assignment of extra work that is unrelated to the act for which the offender is being punished.

Discipline in the Classroom

Discipline is necessary in the classroom in order to carry on instruction. Law and order are as necessary in the classroom as they are essential for the other pursuits in life. Before however, we can determine the methods of obtaining discipline in the classroom, we must discover some of the reasons for indiscipline among children in the classroom.

Group Psychological Factors Operate which Produce Classroom Difficulties

These are the results of an interaction of individual disturbances. The reasons are:

1. Dissatisfaction in the work process.
2. Emotional unrest in interpersonal relations.
3. Disturbances in the group climate.
4. Composition of the group.

Conclusion

The word 'freedom' is used in different contexts. Originally it comes from the word 'free' and is a condition for living. Freedom is also the birth-right of every human being. Man is born free. Nobody likes interference. Thus it is a basic condition for effective functioning. "freedom is a basic need", Kant says that all moral acts may not be free acts. There are limits to freedom. In short freedom may imply both positive and negative concepts. E.g: Freedom from want and fear is more positive as a concept. Freedom in education has a wide connotation. This implies freedom of action on the part of teachers and parents, in school and classroom, at home and in the community.

Discipline enhances the scope of freedom, discipline implies self-restraint. Discipline should be a condition preceeding instruction. Let these be some codes of behaviour established which pupils is expected to follow in the classroom, for learning to take place. Discipline will follow interest and involvement in the learning process: the pupils will co-operate whole-heartedly without creating any behaviour problems.

REFERENCES

1. Aggarwal, J.C. (1985). Theory and Principles of Education. New Delhi: Vikas Pub. (Pvt.) Ltd.
2. Bhatia, K. & Batia, B. (1992). The Philosophical and Sociological Foundations of Education. New Delhi: Doaba House.
3. Bhattacharya (1996). Foundations of Education, New Delhi, Atlantic Publishers, 1996.
4. Edwards, P. (1972). The Encyclopedia of Philosophy. New York: Mc Milan Pub. Co. Inc.
5. Frank (1996). A History of Philosophy. Allahabad: Central Publishing House.
6. Husen, T. & Neville P. The International Encyclopedia of Education, (2nd ed., Vol. 4), U.S.A.: Pergamon.
7. Pandey, R.S. Principles of Education. Agra: Vinod Pustak Mandir.
8. Sharma, S.R. (1997). Practice of Philosophy of Education, New Delhi, Mohit.
9. Singha, S.C. (1990). Dictionary of Philosophy, Delhi: Anmol Publications.

5
Education and Discipline

Meaning of Discipline

S. Balakrishna Joshi writes, 'what is discipline? To put it in a nut shell, it is decent and decorous conduct which contributes to harmony, Joy and success, an exalted sense of responsibility, respect for authority, love for orderliness, eagerness to discharge duties with regularity, promptitude and efficiency, a desire to be agreeable and helpful to others by exercising, if necessary a wholesome check on individual proclinyties and a capacity to maintain equipoise in the face of the most trying circumstances-these constitute discipline."

Discipline from Social Point of View

Discipline viewed from the point of view of society is a means of developing a sense of social conscience in an individual so that he identifies himself with the society and contributes for its betterment to which he belongs.

Discipline and Democracy

Discipline is the essence of democracy. In democracy it is not forced from above. It grows from within. It is based on the realization by the individual of the worth of all other individuals. It is the result of 'training of conscience which consists in the cultivation of good will and the development of moral insight.

To quote the secondary education commission; "Discipline is the fruit, the valuable bye product in the co-operative work willingly undertaken and efficiently completed."

Discipline from Individual Point of View

Discipline viewed from the point of view of an individual is a means of enabling him to bring under control his instinctive usages to reach a position where he willingly and spontaneously identifies himself with the right thing.

"The aim of discipline" in the words of Wleton, "Is the training of the conscience which consists in the cultivation of the good will and development of moral insight."

Discipline and Order

J.E. Brown writes that discipline like honour and peace has almost as many different meanings as it has uses. He defines order as "an out ward semblance of good behaviour not in itself to be despised, since it permits work to be carried on smoothy." To achieve order nothing is needed but an authoritative presence with a voice to match, failing which a strong arm is effective.

Discipline as Great Motive Power

Comenius explains the importance of discipline is the life of a great Didactic. There is a proverb in Bohemia. 'A school without discipline is like a mill without water' and this is very true. For if you withdraw the water from a mill, it stops, and in the same way if you deprive a school of discipline, you take away from it its motive power.

'Why', 'When' and 'How' of Discipline

Comenius thinks that proper punishment is 'like a bitter draught presented for them (children) by the doctor'. Comenius starts with the proposition that punishment should be employed towards those who err. But it is not because they have erred that they should be punished (for what has been done cannot be done), but in order that may not err again in the future.

Discipline should, therefore, be free from personal elements, such as anger or dislike and should be exercised with such frankness and sincerity of purpose, that even the pupils may feel that the action taken is for their good and those get over them are but exercising paternal authority. They will thus regard it in the same light as a bitter draught prescribed for them by the doctor.

Punishment where Morality is at Stake and not for Studies

Skillful and systematic treatment is necessary to instill a love of learning into minds of our pupils. Studies properly organized can convert their idleness into activity and entire all by their pleasantness. Comenius advises us to learn a lesson from nature.

Classification of Disciplinarians

1. Repressionists.
2. Impressionists.
3. Emanicipationists.

1. *Repressionists:* They believe in the 'theory of flogging'. Discipline is enforced from above and is known as 'external discipline'. It is based on fear, force and coercion. A child is loaded by many 'does' and 'donts'.
2. *The Impressionists:* They believe that 'impression' rather than 'repression' should from the basis of discipline. In the words of John Adams, 'Impressionists are those who still seek to dominate but without using the savage way of repression'.
3. *The Emanicipationists:* They believe in the doctrine of 'Laizzez faire' or 'free discipline'. This is the outcome of the teachings of educationists like Roussean, Froebal, Montessori etc. 'Save the Child' is the slogan of these educationists.

Dangers of Unrestricted Freedom

Unregulated freedom can be allowed only at our peril. Bagley rightly puts it as, "the pupil is immature and helpless and he must not be given a long rope with which he may hang himself." Absolute freedom is a myth. It does not exist, did not exist, will not exist and should not exist. Ryburn rightly thinks, "Freedom in school should bear some relation to the freedom that is found in the world at large."

Excessive Restrictions are Equally Bad

A child who is constantly loaded by many 'Do's' and 'Don't's' is unlikely to develop into a well-balanced personality. He will not get sufficient opportunities to do his best. His initiative and drive will be checked. His faculties will remain stunted and creative powers will remain unharnessed. Authority which derives its strength and sanction from fear paralyses the human mind and spirit. The great philosopher Russell writes, "the man whose tongue is constricted by the censorship, whose laws are constricted by an ethic which considers jealousy a better thing than by affection, whose childhood had been imprisoned in the code of manners and whose youth has been drilled in a cruel orthodoxy, will feel against the world that hampers him with the same rage that is felt by the infant whose arms and legs are held motionless. In his rage he will turn to destruction, becoming a revolutionary, a militarist or a persecuting moralist according to temperament and opportunity'.

It is wrong to believe, "what the whip was to do to the horse, the rod was to do to the child."

Internal Discipline

William. A. Yeager, "Historically, it always is associated with the concept of discipline, having the connotations of strict mental, moral and physical training, requiring for its achievement submission to authority, with proper punishment meted out for disobedience in any form. Thus it implies something 'external' that is conformity to an external stimulus or impulse. More recently a school control has come to imply something internal, a response to an inner stimulus or impulse."

Discipline, Authority and Freedom

Any authority has a unifying and stabilizing role. The close connection between authority, freedom, responsibility and discipline has been discussed.

Discipline relates to the mode of behaviour in relation to the accepted and expected norms imposed by the authority. To this extent, the freedom enjoyed by an individual is curtailed for the sake of the larger interests of the system to which the individual belongs.

E.g:- We Indians are enjoying our freedom since 15th August 1947. We are free to govern ourselves as we like. The constitution of India has bestowed on all Indian citizens- the freedom of expression, assembly, freedom of speech and press. That does not mean that there are no constraints on our behaviour. We cannot indulge in any kind of anti-national or antisocial activity. Then the law takes care of it. We must be disciplined Indians, who strive to promote the interests of the nation and society large. Indiscipline of any kind that is detrimental to the interests of our society- or nation will not be tolerated. If we indulge in such things, severe action will be taken against us.

Hence Harry Schofield observed; 'we must have discipline in order to have our freedom, since freedom develops out of and through discipline. Discipline is not a constraint placed upon discipline."

Freedom without discipline leads to a state of anarchy and disorder. We must also learn from our past that due to the indiscipline and excessive freedom, our past Indian rulers enjoyed, the nation had been under the domination of one foreign power or the other for centuries. Discipline imposes control over our freedom and safeguards it from becoming a licence to do anything as we like or to say whatever we want without considering the interests of our society and nation.

Discipline makes us realize the responsibility we should shoulder for sake of the members of the society and for the interest of the nation.

Classification of Discipline

Discipline may be classified in different ways; i.e., as the external or internal, as the normal or abnormal and as the consistent or inconsistent.

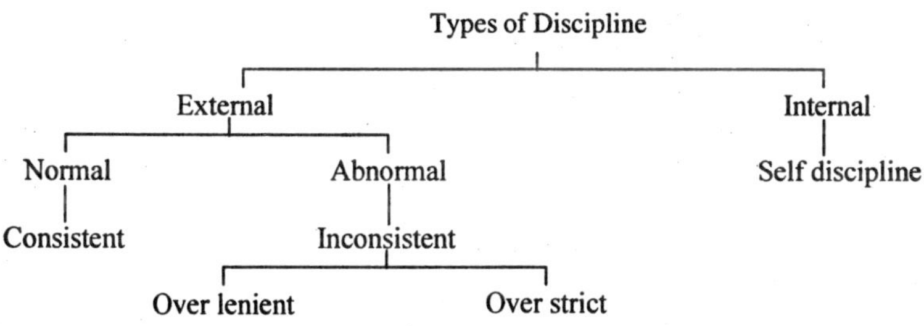

The above types of discipline relates to the overt behaviour of man. There are also other types of discipline which relate to covert behaviour-mental discipline or intellectual discipline. But here our discussion is relates to the overt behaviour only.

Kothari Commission observes, "The discipline which higher education cultivates should aim at self-discipline i.e., discipline directed from within, which does not depend primarily on external control." Self discipline involves self-control and self-direction. There will be voluntary submission to rules in it.

Discipline imposed by the external agencies may be termed to be external. It is considered to be normal if it is consistent and abnormal if inconsistent. In consistent discipline may further be categorized as the over-strict or over-lenient. Both these latter types are not conducive to the development of the desired behaviours in the clientele.

Discipline and Education

Discipline is essential in any educational system to enable it to achieve the desired objectives and goals. Secondary Education Commission: "The real purpose of education is to train youth to discharge the duties of citizenship properly. All other objectives are incidental. Discipline, therefore, should be the responsibility of parents, teachers, the general public and the authorities concerned." According to T.P. Nunn; "discipline is not an external thing like order but something that touches the innermost springs of conduct."

Indiscipline in Schools

Now-a-days indiscipline has become a constant phenomenon in-educational institutions throughout the country. The general causes for student indiscipline may be enumerated as follows:

1. Wide-spread frustration among students.
2. Loss of leadership by the teachers.
3. Degradation of values.
4. Defects of the educational system.
5. Change in the Teacher-pupils relationship.

Discipline and Classroom Management

Discipline is a more specific term and refers to the status of pupil behaviour in the classroom. Thus a class that is said to home good discipline would have all or most of the students, on-task, that is, following directions and generally doing the things the teacher wants them to do when they are supposed to.

Discipline is the required action by a teacher or school official, towards a student (or group of students), after the students behaviour disrupts the ongoing educational activity to break a pre-established rule of law created by the teacher, the educational administration or the general society.

Table–5:1
Causes of Indiscipline and Unrest Among Students

Sl. No.	Factor	Causes
1.	Personal	Mental deficiency
2.	Personal	Physical handicap
3.	Personal	Non-satisfaction of urges
4.	Personal	Frustration
5.	Personal	Mal-adjustment
6.	Personal	Emotional imbalance etc.
7.	Home	Inconsistent discipline
8.	Home	Father-mother quarrels
9.	Home	Improper-attention by parents
10.	Home	Feelings of insecurity at home
11.	Home	Over-growth of the family
12.	Home	Hostile attitude toward parents
13.	Home	Disintegration of families
14.	Home	Low moral standards of home
15.	Home	Lack of formation of moral sentiment
16.	Home	Lack of parental control of children etc.
17.	Society	Influence of politicians
18.	Society	Interference of politicians in schools
19.	Society	Influence of anti-social elements
20.	Society	Influence of crime and sex literature
21.	Society	Influence of romantic and crime films
22.	Society	Lack of education in political ideology
23.	Society	Lack of recreational facilities
24.	Society	Social prejudices
25.	Society	Indoctrination of narrow fanatic views
26.	Society	Religious sanctions
27.	School	Inconsistent discipline in schools
28.	School	Licence of teachers
29.	School	Teacher's negligent attitude towards insubordination.

How to Achieve Self Discipline or Creative Discipline or Democratic Discipline or Social Discipline

1. Placing Responsibility upon Children.
2. Utilization of Abundant Energy of the Youth.
3. Discipline among the Staff Members.
4. A Democratic School Organization.
5. Provision of Recreational Activities.
6. Games.
7. Material Conditions of Work.
8. Methods of Teaching.
9. Sympathetic Attitudes.
10. Personal Relationship.
11. Guidance and Counselling Service.
12. Punishment.
13. Moral Education.
14. Use of Appropriate Knowledge.
15. Appreciation at the Right Time.
16. Deep and Genuine Interest in work.
17. Need for ideal Examples.

Discipline in Various Schools of Philosophy

Idealism and Discipline

Idealism advocates a sort of rigorous discipline which liberates pupils from excessive material wants. It is midway between the repressionism of the autocrats and Emancipation of the extreme nature naturalists. Idealism is inclined toward impressionism, a sort of strict discipline inculcated through high standards of personal conduct. The pupils look with awe and respect their teacher who is thought to be a repository of spiritual knowledge.

Naturalism and Discipline

The naturalist permits freedom for the child to plan his own activities. Children must feel completely free to govern themselves with no direction from above. Hence, naturalists advocates self-government in schools. They believe in disciplining the body and mind by natural consequences. Spencer says, "when a child falls, it suffers pain, the remembrance of which tends to make it more careful; and by repetition of such experiences the child eventually disciplined into proper guidance of its movements." Leaving the child to the discipline of the consequences, is something dangerous. Therefore, modern naturalism is in favour of free discipline, which makes the child self-disciplined with an insight into his duties and responsibilities.

Pragmatism and Discipline

It is the mental attitude produces self discipline. Let the natural interests of children be aroused, satisfied and sustained; and the problem of indiscipline will not arise. Purposeful co-operative activities are conducive to self-discipline. Such activities create values like initiative, self-reliance, toleration, sympathy and fair flay. These values help in building the morals and training the character. In pragmatism there is no place for rewards and punishments. Morals grow from democratic living.

Punishment has a definite place but should be used very carefully, sparingly and judiciously. To quote R.C. Wren, "punishment is an evil thing and a thing to be avoided. So is the surgeon's knife. Both are necessary however." Similarly Bray has observed "punishment is the lesser evil applied to avoid the greater one that lives in the future." The teacher's smile should be reward and frown punishment.

Conclusion

According to J.E. Brown, "A co-operative mental attitude in which each member of the class freely gives of his best because he feels himself a member of a corporate body whose aims are recognized as worthy, and misbehaviour on the part of any member is condemned by the whole body because it is recognized not only or even chiefly as a crime against the central authority, but as an offence against the whole 'community'. The aim of such discipline is to produce self-reliant, self-controlled men and women who will work without supervision. This is the ideal stage and is know as Constructive Discipline."

"Constructive Discipline is the outcome of the activities and experiences that inculcate in the individual virtues of self control based on reason and not on Force. It is the outcome of persuasion and not of compulsion. It comes out of doing rather than of talking. Like religion it cannot be taught but can only be caught and practiced."

REFERENCES

1. Bhatacharya, S. (1996). *Foundations of Education*. New York: Atlantic Publishes.
2. Aggarwal, J.C. (1992). *Theory and Principals of Education*. New Delhi: Vikas Publishing House (P) Ltd.
3. Monore, P. (2000). *Encyclopaedia of Philosophy of Education*. New Delhi: Cosmo Publications.
4. Taneja, V.R. (1987). *Educational Thought and Practice*. New Delhi Sterling Publishers (P) Ltd.
5. Bhatia, K. (1992). *Theory and Principles of Education*. New Delhi Doaba House.
6. Sindhu, K.S. (1997). *School Organization and Administration* (3rd Ed.). New Delhi: Sterling Publishers (P) Ltd.
7. Nair, V. (Ed) & Sudharma, A. (2002). '*Emerging Facets of Education*'. Thiruvananthapuram: Literacy Forum.

6

Bhagawad Gita and Education

Introduction

Shreemadbhagawad Gita is an epitome of the Vedic culture and literature. It is the essence of all Indian scriptures. In this unique holy book we find a clear analysis of the various Yogas. The relationship between the Jeeva (the being) and Ishwar (God) has been clearly explained in the Yoga, viz., Karma Yoga, Bhakti Yoga and Gyan Yoga. All these three types have been clearly defined in Gita. But how has it been possible to envelop the various Yogas in such a short book? It may be said that Gita covers all the scriptures (Shastras). It is a wonderful collection of boundless ideas and feelings (Bhava). It is because of these boundless ideas that the various commentators have succeeded in propounding various 'isms' and ideas. Shri Shankaracharya has advocated Gyan Yoga through his commentary on Gita. Shri Ramanujacharya has propounded Bhaktiyoga on Gita. Lok Manya Tilak has considered Gita chiefly as Karmayoga.

Exploration of the Basic Elements of Life

1. *The Chief Motivation Free of Life*

We do not live in a vaccum. We reside in a very wide environment which is full of complexities and intricacies. There is always an inevitable interaction between us and the environment. This interaction is a sign of life. Every living being is subjected to this interaction. Of course, variations are found in the interactions of various living creatures. A dog seeing a monkey reacts in a certain way, but the human baby seeing a monkey becomes excited and shows different reactions. In the nature of on there is an element of intelligence. This element brings in change in the situation. Due to his intelligence, man is not bound to follow a certain path. He is able to make a choice from various alternatives before him. This ability of making a choice creates for him a complex problem. Now arises the issue of policy. The exploration of elements of life attempts to resolve the arisen issue.

Arjun places his difficulty before Krishna who expresses his view point for helping him to solve his difficulty. The battle between Kauravas and Pandavas was to begin. Armies of both the parties were present in the battle ground of Kurukshetra. Krishna brought the chariot with Arjun in between the two armies. As a signal to start the battle, drums were beaten and Shankhas (conches) were blown. Now a doubt arises in Arjun's mind whether to fight or not to fight. Arjun was a Kshatriya. It was his duty to fight. But the doubt arose because of the uniqueness of the situation. In a battle one party is an enemy of another and wants to destroy it. In Kurukshetra close relations were standing before each other. The family bond duty was not to shed blood of each other, but at the same time 'duty' warranted that the prestige must be also maintained. In the very beginning of Gita, Kurukshetra has been termed as Dharmaskhetra (i.e., the place of performing sacred duties). Now there is a clash between the blood-relationship and the Dharma. i.e., the duty, Arjun is not able to decide his course of action. The morality viewpoint arises and the policy is now that of morality. When there is a policy matter, there are alternatives.

Arjun tells Krishna, what is the use of Kingdom which is to be obtained by killing close relations consisting of elders and revered persons? It is better to earn a living through begging. Arjun further asks Krishna: "What is the certainty of our victory in the battle? Should we then shed blood in this uncertain situation?" Now Krishna says, "Arjun, why are you expressing this ignorance? This conduct is neither praiseworthy nor can it lead you to heaven, nor will it give you glory."

Krishna says, "Oh Arjun you say that so many relatives will be killed. But the fact is that you, I and all others were present previous to this birth and we shall remain even after this life is finished.

The one who thinks that he can kill a soul, and the one who considers it as dead, both do not know. The soul neither kills nor is it killed" (2-19).

Even if soul is under bondage of birth and death even then death is no cause of grief. All these have to die, just there is a difference after or before (2-26).

To desist from battle is not noble. Battle is your life mission. If a warrior dies as a duty, the heaven's doors become open for him.

For a Kshatriya there is nothing higher than dying for a righteous (Dharmayudha) battle (2-3-2).

Your argued cause for desisting for battle is unheavenly. If you do not fight you lose both glory and your duty (Swadharma). All will decry you. And for a good man infamy is worse than death. And who will know that you left the battle ground for love of your relatives. All will say that you have run away from the battle due to fear.

You say that you do not know whether you will win or lose in the battle, but at least you know this that if you are killed you will go to heaven and if you win you will get the Kingdom (2-31-37).

Giving the above reasoning Krishna says to Arjun. "Treat gain and loss, victory and defeat as the same thing, get ready for battle. By doing this you will be committing no sin" (2-38).

The main substance of the entire reasoning of Krishna in this is that if duty (Dharma) draws one side and another motivating force to another, then in every situation one should act according to duty (Dharma). The demand of duty is above everything else. This idea is an original concept of moral education in Gita.

Krishna says that to treat gain and loss, and 'victory and defeat' as equal is extremely difficult. Pleasure and pain are experienced in the present, harvesting the benefit of gain and victory is matter for future. In accepting guidance of the intellect, the main obstruction is from the attachment of the outcome. In Gita several times it has been observed that one should be indifferent (Udasin) to attachment and outcome. A duty should be performed with the feeling of doing a duty.

The philosopher Kant of Germany has also accepted the above view point of Gita. He has also said that in the performance of one's duty, one should be indifferent to attachment and outcome.

2. *The Door of Hell*

When the attachment (Bhava) is a very powerful, and it is not momentary, then it is called wordly pleasures (Vishaya). Five wordly pleasures are famous. They are lust (Kam), anger (Krodh), Greed (Lobha), delusion (Moha) and Pride (Ahamkar). Lust, anger and greed are regarded as doors to hell. In the face of these, the intellect becomes very weak. In all stories lust (Kam) has been considered as blind. When in just, a person does not look either forward on backward. Anger is generated when justful desire is not fulfilled. In greed, the intellect, being powerless, becomes a handmaid to attachment and becomes helpful in realizing the objective. In greed one wants to enjoy the fruit of another man's labour, in the same way as it is the horse who runs, but it is rider who reaches the destination. In human being greed is a powerful casue of friction. The domain of greed is much wider than of lust and anger.

3. *The Path Towards Fall*

In Gita lust (Kam) has been given the first place in the doors of hell. The word lust may be used both in narrow and in wider sense. Within the wider sense all types of desires are included in it. A desire or Kama is a basic motivation in human nature. When a desire is unfulfilled we become unhappy and if possible, we attempt to remove all the obstacles in the way of realizing the same. If our attempt is very risk, we get anger also. Desire is an element our human nature. But the things that come within the objectives of our desire are not definite in the beginning. They may be very few or many and of varying nature. The thing for which one has an attachment may not be within the desires of another person. When we feel attachment for a certain thing that enters into our consciousness and gradually we become more and more conscious about it. When we fail in achieving our desire we get anger. In anger the intellect becomes covered and we are not able to see the concerned thing in the right perspective. What is the reason for this inability?

A thing that we happen to see is not in a vaccum. That thing is encircled by other things which are continually influencing it. This kind of action and reaction is an element of its existence. Nothing is momentary. That which appears to be momentary has its past also. When we thing about a thing we are also related with things that are related with it. When Arjun expressed his difficulty before Krishna, his intellect could understand the situation in its various aspects. He was reminded of the blood-relationships and of his attachment for Bhishma and great regard for his Guru Dronacharya. At this time his intellect was working. He know that when engaged in the battle he forget all these things. In anger, a person forgets the past and does not think above future. When a person reaches this stage, his intellect vanishes and he comes up at the brink of all (2-62-3).

4. *The Significance of Self-Duty (Swadharma)*

Krishna tells Arjun that a duty (Swadharma) has to be performed for the sake of duty itself. The desire for outcome and attachment pulls down the work from the moral view point. It is said in Gita that it is excellent if one performed his duty, even if the work done is lower than that of any other person. Even to die is auspicious while performing one's duty, to act according to another person's duty is dreadful (3:35).

Educational Implications of Gita

1. *The True Meaning of Education*

We may derive the true meaning of education through the virtuous knowledge (Satwika Gyan) as emphasized by Krishna (18:20). Virtuous knowledge is that through which we perceive unity in diversity and sense the Brahma (i.e., God or Parmeshwar) in all the creatures on this earth. Thus we may accept according to the philosophy of Gita that true education is that which helps one to see the existence of God (i.e., Brahma) in the soul of an individual. Arjun was delusioned at the start of the battle. Krishna (his Guru) helps him to see the whole epitomized in one individual, Krishna, i.e., God Himself. Thus Krishna tries to help Arjun to see the point that he (Arjun) cannot kill any one's soul which resides in the Brahma (God) Himself.

2. *The Ideals of Education*

We may analyze the ideals of education into six parts, such as:

- *(a)* To develop virtuous knowledge.
- *(b)* To develop and effect sublimation of personality.
- *(c)* To co-ordinate between the individual and social aim.
- *(d)* To develop the inner consciousness.
- *(e)* To develop intellectual and logical ability.
- *(f)* To establish the importance of duty in life.

Now we try to understand how Gita refers to the above ideals of education.

(a) To Develop Virtuous Knowledge

Our students, like all of us, suffer from ignorance of virtuous knowledge. In Gita Krishna removes Arjun's ignorance and motivates his towards performing his duty. From this position we may take up the idea that the ideal of education should be to remove ignorance and to provide the virtuous knowledge.

(b) To Develop and Effect Sublimation of Personality

Everyone's personality is equipped with evil (Asuri) and virtuous (Daivi-godly) traits. In other words, Kauravas (Asuri) and Pandavas (the virtuous) exist in each of us. Krishna awakens in Arjun the virtuous powers inherent in him and motivates him towards the right path. This is exactly what a Guru should do for his disciple. Thus the ideal of education should be to develop and sublimate the personality of the student.

(c) To Co-ordinate Between the Individual and Social Aim

In the battle-field Arjun is lost between his individual freedom and the social responsibility. His individual freedom was to fight or not to fight. The social responsibility warranted his participation in the battle for punishing the evil-doors for establishing peace in the land. Krishna impresses upon him to sacrifice his individual freedom and take up the Gandeev for annihilating the wicked persons and their allies. Thus we may say that according to Gita 'one of the chief ideals of education should be to effect a co-ordination between the individual and social aspects of things'.

(d) To Develop the Inner Consciousness

Arjun desires to keep himself away from the ghastly battlefield. Krishna does not want to force him against his will. Instead, he (Krishna) takes recourse to logical reasoning and tries to convince Arjun about his sacred self-duty (Swadharma). Ultimately, on his own, Arjun decides to fight against his opponents. Thus Krishna, his Guru and Friend, succeeds in awakening the inner consciousness (Anthahakaran). This is exactly the ideal that we should follow in the fields of education.

(e) To Develop Intellectual and Logical Ability

Arjun expresses his doubt regarding the utility of battle. His doubt is at the root of preachings of Gita. Krishna employs his intellectual and logical ability for removing Arjun's doubt. Thus the main purpose of the philosophy of Gita is to develop the intellectual and logical ability of Arjun (the common man) in order that he may be able to take his own decision in the face of alternatives. This should be our ideal of education also.

(f) To Establish the Importance of Duty

One can be happy only by establishing a balance between one's rights and duties. Krishna tells Arjun that nothing is greater than performance of one's duty (Swadharma-Palan). It is very necessary to emphasize this viewpoint before the students of these days. If our students develop this attitude towards life, then this very earth will become a heaven.

3. *The Curriculum*

Gita refers to two types of knowledge (Gyan)—*(i)* the Apara Vidya, i.e., the knowledge about mundane affairs and *(ii)* the Para Vidya, i.e., the spiritual knowledge or the knowledge about the supreme self. In the knowledge about mundane affairs we may include all types of subjects in various disciplines of arts, science and engineering etc. which are generally taught in our education centres. Within the Para Vidya—the spiritual realm-is generally ignored. This was resulted in the predominance of acquisition of worldly wealth of various types at the utter neglect of spiritual realm. The knowledge about the spiritualism alone can give eternal peace to man. Hence in our educational system. "the spiritual aspects of man's life should also be given its due place along with subjects related with worldly affairs."

4. *The Concept of Moral Education According to Gita*

In the foregoing pages we have said that the performance of one's duty (Swadharma-Palan) has been principally emphasizes in Gita. It was towards the fulfillment of this ideal that Arjun takes the decision to fight in the battle-field. Krishna has impressed upon him that one's duty should be performed without taking into consideration its outcome and attachment (Rag) for the same. It is extremely difficulty to think of any higher moral ideal for a man than this. Through practicing this ideal a person will reach the peak of his development and he will overcome all worldly attachment. This is exactly what is needed in our youths to these days. So if we impress upon them to practice the above ideal with shall be giving them the noblest moral education.

Conclusion

Because of his intelligence, man can make a choice, when faced against various alternatives. The choice is to be made according to one's study. No desire of outcome and attachment. Gita helps a person to see the existence of God in all creatures. Education to develop virtuous knowledge, personality, inner consciousness, intellectual and logical ability and importance of duty in one's life. Along with knowledge of mundane affairs, spiritual knowledge to be imparted.

REFERENCES

1. Mohanty, J. (1982). *Indian Education in the Emerging Society*, New Delhi: Sterling Publishers.
2. Radhakrishnan, S. & Moore. *Source Book of Indian Philosophy*. Allen and Uncoin.
3. Rena, R. (1971). *Introduction to Indian Philosophy*. New Delhi: Tala Mac Graw Hill.
4. Rusk R. & Robert. (1951). *A History of Indian Education*. London: University of London Press.
5. Sharma, R.N. (2000). *Text Book of Educational Philosophy*. New Delhi: Kanishka Publishers, Distributors.
6. Vivekananda (1982). *Complete Works of Swami Vivekananda* (Vol. V). Advits Publishers.

7

Educational Importance of Upanishads and Bhagawad Gita

Introduction

Education is a growing science and its foundations are to be explored for a study of the subject as an inter-disciplinary approach. Philosophy is the corner stone of the foundation of Education. But thus does not mean that education should be enslaved to philosophy or some set of values created by human society. Philosophy should be interpreted as a vision in a wider prospective. This being so, education should be wedded to some philosophy in general. We need some frames of reference in which education has to fit. There have been various schools of philosophy presenting their views with much optimism. Education is the process of enabling people not merely do live but to live adequately. There are various facts of education: academic, aesthetic, moral, physical, social and spiritual. Theories of education have been formulated and different values emphasized.

Every educational practice is illuminated with the backdrop of philosophy. The speculative, normative and critical function of philosophy affects not only the direction of moral guidance that the teacher gives but also affects the direction of moral guidance that the teacher gives but also affects the direction and the emphasis of the curriculum, the colour of the teachers attitudes from day to day, even from hour to hour.

Education in the Vedic Period

The present education has its roots deeply embedded in the past. India's has been singularly glorious. Its refulgence has not only in the present but also aroused faith in the future. In the ancient period, all the political, economic and social current emanated from spiritualism. Social life was solidly founded upon good conduct, love, non-violence etc. Co-operation and co-existence formed its spirit. The fundamental unit of society was the individual.

Education in India had its beginnings in the need to satisfy man's innate curiosity, while he lived in the lap of nature. It is usually argued that the elements, methodology and organization of education in India originated during the vedic period. India's educational and cultural traditions are the most ancient in the world's history. In ancient India, the tradition of society and the nation were preserved in schools. India's ancient period has been so glorious and rich that foreign scholars have praised it lavishly.

Characteristic of education are – knowledge, aims of education, the method of education, the 'upanayana' ritual, celibacy or brahmacharya, service of the teacher, accepting aims, practicality education for the individual, duration of education, curriculum, method of teaching, relations between student and teacher, women's education, vocational education, educational achievements etc.

Upanishads

The word Upanishad means sitting near devotedly. It brings to the mind the picture of co earnest disciple or learner learning from his spiritual "guru" or teacher. Apart from Indian scholars and seers, European also have sung the glory of the Upanishads. The Upanishads deal with knowledge (vidya) destroys ignorance (avidya) and takes the seeker to salvation (moksha) and to Brahma (God) and help him to understand him in the true sense and thus liberates him from the bondage of the world (Freedom from the cycle of births and deaths). The Upanishads are recognized as 'Shruthi' or Revelation. The total number of Upanishads are 108. Ten are the most important among them.

Educational Implications

Educational implications of Upanishads may be worked out keeping in view aims, content, methodology, school administration and other educational process.

Aims of Education

Education during Upanishadic period was related to social norms and it tried to conserve the cultural tradition of the society of those days. The society was divided on the basis of 'Varanas' and 'Ashramas'. But education did not only conserve that social ethos, it is also bring about social change. Aim of education are summarized as follows:

(a) Character building
(b) Development of personality
(c) Knowledge of social roles and status
(d) Vocational efficiency
(e) National integration.

The Content

The content was related to the needs of individual and society. Philosophy, Theology, History, Geography, Astronomy, Astrology, Arithmatic, Algebra, Geometry, Language, Literature, Ayurveda, Dhanurveda and the like were taught and learnt by Upanishadic philosophers and students. Psychology was being studied with greater interest.

Methodology

Methods of Upanishadic philosophy analyzed by Prof. R.D. Ranade in to ten categories-Etymological method, Mythical method, Dialectic method, Synthetic method... etc. All the above method of teaching was discovered by Upanishadic philosophers according to the need of the hour. They were suited to the content of education and educational goals.

Teaching was done at that time at all the three levels viz., memory understanding and reflective. The emphasis was laid on discussions, questioning, induction and deduction. Commentaries, illustrations, descriptions, narrations and practical demonstrations may be easily inferred from the text of Upanishads.

System of Education

The teacher pupil relationship was ideal. A teacher taught about 15 to 20 pupils at a time he was prepared to teach even one pupil. The pupil was well disciplined, courteous, modest and humble. He pleased the teacher by his service as well as through study.

Sanskrit was the medium of instruction and oral discussion formed the basis of teaching-learning which were suplimented by text-books in post-literacy period. The schools were of three types. Firstly, ashramas or 'Gurukulas' which may be said to be primary schools, 'charanas' may be compared roughly with our secondary schools and 'parishads' were meant for higher studies and researches. Upanishads contain doctrines of self realization and the implication is that both teachers and students were devoted to learning, study, meditation through which they tried to realize the self.

The Teachers of Upanishadic Period

The teachers who lived, thought and taught in the Upanishadic period made real contribution to the development of Upanishadic thought. Some of the teachers who are mentioned in Upanishads do not seem to be historical personalities. They are mythological personages. For example, Indra, Virochana, Prajapati, Varuna, Yama seem to be unhistorical persons.

None of some great teachers (historical persons) are Svetasvatara, Trishanku, Mantri, Kaushitaki, Uddalaku, Ajatsatru, Vamadeva, Sandilya, Sanatakumara, Aruni, Vajnavalkya...etc.

The Upanishadic teachers were the symbols of "simple living and high thinking." They were embodiment of character and knowledge. They may be source of inspiration to the teachers of all the places and at all the times.

The Student-Teacher Relationship

The Guru and his wife had to perform respectively the role of the father and that of the mother for the disciple accepted in the Gurukul. The pupil accepted the teacher and his father and mother as well, and he never dared to oppose him in any way. The Manusmirit explains this relationship thus in a clear manner — 'A dwija is born twice. First after his mothers conception and secondly at the time of his initiation ceremony when he is made fit to acquire the knowledge of the Brahma.

The Guru also performed his duty honestly. He taught his student the truth exactly as he knew it. He never concealed anything from his disciple. The disciple also did not conceal his weakness from his Guru.

Implications of the Upanishadic Era for Modern Education

The importance of the Upanishadic Era for modern education are–the ideal of development of the whole man, the ideal of good moral character, the concepts of the ideal teacher and the ideal student, the high ideals of the Upanishadic Gurus to be achieved, college and universities, hostels to be repatterned on the great Upanishadic ideals of Gurukula and the Upanishadic ideals for modern students.

The Ideal of Development of the Whole Man

We have seen in the foregoing pages that the educational system during the Upanishadic period stood for on all-sided development of the pupil in such a way that he realized himself as a full man and ultimately attained immortality. Educationalist like Mahatma Gandhi, Rabindranath Tagore, Swami Vivekananda and many others in our country have also emphasized the ideal of the development of the whole man. But the words of our wise men have not made any impact on our modern educational system. With the result that today we happen to see many stinted specimens of humanity in the forms of graduates of our colleges and universities.

The Ideal of Good Moral Character

An ideal man doesn't not live for himself alone. The aim of education during the Upanishadic age was also to enable the pupil to develop himself in such a manner that he might contribute to the development of society. He find the practice of highest moral ideal during the Upanishadic period. Today many of our youths happen to be misguided as to work as social miscreants disturbing the peace of our society. So we must incorporate in our modern educational system the ideal of high moral character.

The Concepts of the Ideal Teacher and the Ideal Student

We have seen in the foregoing pages that the Upanishadic Guru assumed the roles of ideal teachers and they derived spiritual pleasure in helping their pupils to understood the truth of human existence. In our modern educational system we have to incorporate the concept of ideal teacher and the ideal pupil.

The High Ideals of the Upanishadic Gurus to be Achieved

Our modern teacher education colleges preparing teachers for schools profess to develop in the trainees the ideals which were actually praised by the Upanishadic preceptors. Many of the educational departments of the various universities in our country have fallen short of everything that are desirable for an ideal teacher.

College and Universities to be Repatterned on the Great Upanishadic Ideals of Gurukula

During the Upanishadic period the house of the preceptor (the Guru or Acharya) used to function as a residential university for pupils who were there for seeking the *Aparavidya.* The modern colleges and universities having hostels are now no more centres of learning. In order to make them ideal residential centres for our students we should look towards the great grand traditions of the Gurukuls of the Upanishadic age and remodel them on the same pattern under the strict supervision of some really good teachers.

The Upanishadic Ideals for Modern Students

The pupils during the Upanishadic age were admitted to a Gurukul of the preceptor's Ashram after his deservingness was fully tested by the preceptor. Today many students join college and universities in order to become film-stars. Today students come to college and universities to learn new fashions. Our students may be saved from these undesirable things if we assimilate the ideals and principles followed by the Upanishadic preceptors.

Education in the vedic period is:

1. Education was conducted in the gurukul or teacher's house
2. Students lived as members of a family
3. The emphasis was upon the study of the Vedas
4. Sanskrit was the median of education
5. Brahmanas were the teachers
6. Education was not available to every class of society
7. The students life was rigorous
8. Education was free
9. Sanskrit was taught.

Upanishads sources of all Indian philosophies. It means knowledge and for salvation knowledge about self is necessary. In modern education, the concept of the ideal teacher and the ideal student to be incorporated. The student should learn the Upanishadic ideals to build the highest form of moral character for the social good.

Bhagavad Gita and Education

Bhagavad Gita is a part of Mahabharatha. It consists of 700 couplets in 18 chapters. The relation of Gita and the Upanishads has been only too well-known to the Indian philosophers. According to the Vaishaviya Tantrasara "The Upanishads are like cow, Krishna like a milkman, Arjuna like the calf that is sent to the udders of the cow before milking and the Bhagavad Gita like the milk-rector that is churned from the udders of the cow." Thus it has been traditionally well-known that Gita is the essence of the philosophy of the Upanishads. Gita is helpful to the ordinary man in understanding his duties. Thus Gita has a very important place in Indian Philosophy.

Principal teaching of Gita is

- Doing duty as dharma
- Death is certain
- Soul is immortal
- Incarnations
- Social welfare
- Karmayoga
- Two ways of liberation
- Renunciation on attitude of mind etc.

Educational Implications of Gita

The main implication of Gita is—True meaning of education, objectives of education and pupil teacher relationship.

The True Meaning of Education

The true meaning of education through the virtuous knowledge as emphasized by Krishna. True education is that which helps one to see the existence of God in the soul of an individual. Arjun was delusioned of the start of the battle. Krishna helps him to see two whole epitomized in one individual. Thus Krishna tries to help Arjun to see the point that he cannot kill any one's soul which resides in the Brahma himself.

The Ideal of Education

The ideal of education into six parts, such as:

1. To develop virtuous knowledge - our students suffer from ignorance of various knowledge. In Gita Krishna removes

Arjuna's ignorance and motivates him towards performing his duty. It from this position we many take up the idea that the ideal of education should be remove ignorance and to provide the virtuous knowledge.

2. To develop and effect sublimation of personality- Everyone's personality is equipped with evil and virtuous traits. Kauravas and Pandavas exist in each of us.
3. To co-ordinate between the individual and social aim.
4. To develop the inner consciousness.
5. To develop intellectual and logical ability.
6. To establish the importance of duty are the ideal of education.

The Curriculum

Gita refers to two types of knowledge – the *Paravidya* and *Aparavidya*. The knowledge about spiritualism alone can give eternal peace to man. Hence in an educational system "the spiritual aspects of man's life should be given its due place along with subjects related with worldly affairs."

The Concept of Moral Education According to Gita

In the forgoing pages we have said that the performance of one's duty has been principally emphasized in Gita. It was the fulfillment of this ideal that Arjun takes the decision to fight in the battle-field. Through practicing this ideal a person will reach the peak of his development and he will overcome all worldly attachment. This is exactly what is needed in our youths of these days. We impress upon them to practice the above ideal we shall be giving them the noblest moral education.

Gita helps a person to see the existence of God in all creatures. Education to develop virtuous knowledge personality, innerconsciousness, intellectual and logical ability and importance of duty in one's life. Along with knowledge of mundane affairs, spiritual knowledge to be imparted.

Education should aim at acquisition of supreme knowledge and complete development. In modern education, the concept of the ideal teacher and the ideal student to be incorporated. The student should learn the Upanishadic ideals to build the highest form of moral character for the social good. Gita helps a person to see the existence of God in all creatures.

REFERENCES

1. J.C. Aggarwal—*Teacher and Education in a Developing Society.*
2. R.N. Sharma—*History of Indian Philosophy.*
3. Ram Shakal Pandey—*A Survey of Educational Thought.*
4. S.P. Chaube—*Foundations of Education.*
5. Suresh Bhatnagar—*Indian Education Today and Tomorrow.*

8

Educational Prescriptions of Islam as Evidenced through Quran

Introduction

The Arabic word Islam literally means 'Surrender' or 'Submission'. i.e., "Submission to God." Thus one who has surrendered is a Muslim. In theory, all that is necessary for one to become a Muslim is to recite sincerely the short statement of faith known as the "Shahadah." *I witness that there is no god but God (Allah) and that Muhammad is the messenger of God.*

Although in a historical sense Muslims regard their religion as dating from the time of Muhammad in the early 7th century AD, in a religious sense they see it as identical with the true monotheism which prophets before Mohammad, such as Abraham, Moses and Jesus had bought. The followers of these and other prophets are held to have corrupted their teachings, but God in his mercy sent Muhammad to call mankind yet again to the truth.

> "We have not sent there (But as a Messenger) *To all mankind*, giving them Glad tidings and warning them (against Sin), but most men know not" (Qur'an, 34: 28)

Qur'an

Qur'an (Arabic, Al-Qur'an), the chief sacred text of Islam. The Arabic name indicates something 'read' or 'recited'. It contains the revelations made by Allah (God) to Muhammad during his career as a prophet in Mecca and Medina in the first decades of the 7th Century.

The Qur'an is divided into 114 chapters (Suras), each known by a different title. The chapters are divided into verses (Ayas).

The Qur'an's Importance and Interpretation

Qur'an is regarded as one of the two main sources of Islamic law (the other being the Sunnah, the divinely guided behaviour and practice of the prophet).

Much of the work of interpretation is concerned with the occasions of revelation. The individual versus and groups of verses are related to the life of Muhammad and are understood as having been revealed in connection with specific incidents in this life or to solve particular problems which he faced. Thus the text is understood as having an immediate context in the life of Muhammad as well as more universal and timeless significance.

Qur'an begins with Iqrah (Recite), "Recite in the name of your lord who created, created man from Blood congealed. Recite! Your Lord is the most beneficent, who taught by the pen, taught men that which they did not know..."

Qur'an was not authored by Muhammad or by any other human being Muhammad was an illiterate, unable to read or write and remained so till his death.

What is Qur'an About?

The Qur'an, the last revealed word of God, is the primary source of every Muslim's faith and practice. It deals with all the subjects which concern human beings: Wisdom, doctrine, worship, transactions, law etc. but its basic theme is the relationship between God and His creatures. It provide guidelines for a just society, proper human conduct and an economic system.

Knowledge According to Islam

Prophet Muhammed says, "He who goes out in search of knowledge is in God's path till he returns." "The search of knowledge is an obligation laid on every Muslim" (Hadith)."The one who would have the worst position in God's sight on the Day of Resurrection would be a learned man who did not profit from his learning" (Hadith).

The basis of knowledge, according to Islam, is through *Vahia* (revelations); which is revealed through messengers of God. At the age of forty, Muhammad received his first revelation from God through the Angel Gabriel. The revelations continued for 23 years, and they are collectively known as the Qur'an. A person can acquire knowledge through Ijthihad. i.e., a person has the freedom to acquire new knowledge. The source of these acquired knowledge is human imagination and sensory experience. Social science, natural science and applied science are all included in this.

The classification of knowledge is both logical and psychological, because the first, knowledge acquired through revelation, is on the basis of faith and second, acquired knowledge through imagination and sensory experience, is acquired through inspirational faith and human resources.

Acquired knowledge is only temporal in nature whereas knowledge acquired through revelation stands as the ultimate truth. Prophet Mohammed says, "If anyone pursues a path in search of knowledge, God will thereby make easy for his a path to paradise."

How to Acquire Knowledge

> "And Allah brought you out of your mother's wombs devoid of all knowledge, but he has endowed you with hearings and sights, and minds-hearts, so that you may be graceful" (Quran, 16:78).

In the above verses three words "Sama", "Basar" and "Fu'ad" are used for the three faculties of hearing, seeing and thinking. Hearing is through the ears, seeing is through the eyes and thinking is through heart and mind.

Sama means to procure the information and knowledge acquired by others. Basar means to acquire information and knowledge oneself through observation Fu'ad means to extract results by compiling, analyzing and interpreting the information and knowledge procured by Sama and acquired by Basar.

Those who utilize these three faculties collectively with much enthusiasm and vigour. They are dominant and they emerge in this world as leaders.

Aim of Islamic Education

1. The educational system should be in such a way that the learner should attain the status of the representative of God. Behold, thy Lord said to the angels;
   "I will create a vicegerent on earth" (Qur'an 2: 30)
2. It should aim at the development or growth of a balanced

personality through training of soul, intellect, reason, emotions and senses. It helps him to attain the title of "Khaleefathullah."

3. Education should satisfy spiritual, intellectual, physical, scientific and linguistic aptitudes and thus paving the way for his complete development.
4. Basic aim of education is the submissal of oneself to the wish of God in his personal, social and humanistic spheres.
5. Educational system should be moulded in such a way that it should bring dynamism in society.
6. All should get equal opportunity for growth and development as according to his own ability and intellect.
7. Education should provide the learner as the true servant of God to guide himself and the universe and it should not happen by entering a conflict against nature.
8. As a means of plunging into the mysteries of the universe and as a means of opening up the mind to the love and awe towards God, education in theory and practice should encourage self-restraint, self purification and for the cultivation of holiness (sacredness) in our mind.

Prophet Mohammed says, Nawas bin Saman told that; he asked God's Messenger about righteousness and sin and he replied, "Righteousness is good character and sin is that which revolves is your heart and about which you do not want people to know."

Women's Education

The importance of women's education needs to be emphasized. It is as important as men's education. A community cannot progress unless it provides the best education to women, who constitute a vital segment of communal life.

The programme for women's education must be designed in accordance with the teachings of Islam. It must be clearly understood that Islamic culture is totally different from western culture. In the west, a women is not entitled to any right or honour unless she succeeds in performing the functions of a man. Islam on the other hand protects her rights and confers dignity upon her as a woman. It assigns her those responsibilities which suit her feminine nature. As for co-education, there is no scope for it in an Islamic education system at any level.

The primary responsibility of a woman is to look after her home and family, as well as to rear worthy children. The education for women should therefore equip them to discharge these responsibilities efficiently.

Islam and Science

> And they say; "What is there but our life in this world; we shall die and we live and nothing but time can destroy us" But of that they have no knowledge: they merely conjecture. (Quran, 45: 24)

It is regarded that modern science as absolute and true religion, and want to impose this views to all humankind. In other words '*experimental knowledge*' is the unique guide for mankind, experimental knowledge is the knowledge that can be proved or disproved through experiment.

According to this belief of science, all religious information is considered as unreal and questionable. For this reason modern science considers the existence of Allah, the existence of the hereafter are questionable, because they can neither be proved nor observed through an experiment. "Science and Religion have their different fields and should not interfere one another."

This science-religion balance isolates humanity from religion, because humanity can be explained by "experimental knowledge and observation." These remains only two limited areas for religion which are personal ethics and belief. Quran says, "Say: Truly my prayer and my service of sacrifice, my life and my death, Are (all) for Allah, The cherisher of the worlds (Quran: 6: 162).

Islam is a complete way of life and it interfere in all the activities in which man engage. Islam and logic are not in the opposite poles.

The Real Meaning of Science

There is no constant universal science above religion, cultures and ideologies. Science is not a universal guide, certainly, science is guided. For e.g: Newton's scientific hypothesis is a scientific paradigm. With the rise of Einstein's paradigm that is valid today, Newton's paradigm lost its validity. Paradigm is nothing but conjecture that is accepted to be true for a temporary period of time.

According to Paul Feyerabend it is absolutely the result of a subjective preference to consider science as being superior than any other teaching that human kind has put forward. Therefore the government should give up the education policy that regards science as the guide and assumes it is superior than other branches.

Science is neither a guide, nor an aim within itself, but only a tool—a tool that can be used in favour of an intention.

Method: Science and Islam

While most other substances contract when they are cooled, water expands as it freezes. Ice, being less dense than water, flows on it. This fact can be described differently by two persons. An atheistic scientist describes this scientific fact as being essentially inherent in the quality of water, whereas a God-fearing scientist describes this scientific phenomenon as the manifestation of divine wisdom to make life possible in the rivers and seas. The two approaches build different impression on the minds of students. The one approach is intended to undermine the existence of Allah and his providence, whereas the other approach strengthens belief in the existence of Allah and His providence. Instruction along the first line will produce atheistic scientists. Where as instruction along the second line will produce Good-fearing scientists.

Conclusion

Islam is not a religion and Mohammad is not the founder of Islam. It is a total and unified way of life it is a set of beliefs and a way of worship; it is a vast and integrated system of law; it is a culture and civilization; it is an economic system and a way of doing business; it is a polity and a method of governance; it is a special sort of society and a way of running a family; it prescribes for inheritance and divorce, dress and etiquette, food and personal hygiene. It is a spiritual and human totality, this worldly and other-worldly.

REFERENCES

1. Kabir, H. (1955). *Science, Democracy and Islam*. London: Allen and Unwin.
2. Nakosteen, M. (1968). *History of Islamic Organize of Western Education*. Roulder: University of Colorado Press.
3. Paratte, R. (1977). *Ideology and Education*. New York: McDay.
4. Warnock, M. (1977). *Schools of Thought*. London: Faber and Faber.
5. http://www.answers.com

9

Christian Thoughts as Evidenced through 'Bible' and their Influence on Education

Introduction

The Bible is the name given to Christian scriptures. The word Bible is derived from Greek through Latin, which means the books or the roots. It consists of old 'Testament' and the New Testament. Old testament was mostly in Hebrew language written during six or seven hundred years and completed before 150 BC. It contains thirty nine books incorporating traditions, stories and records of sematic tribes of Egypt and Palestine. David and Solomon were powerful kings of this area. Old Testament Contains history, myth, instruction, legislation, prophecy etc. It is written in prose as well as in poetry. The concept of 'covenant' is very important in these books. It is a kind of special relationship between man and God. In convenant, God expressed his choice of Israelite people. Wandering of people between Egypt and Palestine from the part of old Testament which is divided into three sections viz., the Law, the prophets and writings. The law is found in first five books attributed to Moses. The Hebrew word for law is Torah. Laws relating to nomad shepherd life and also to settled agricultural life are contained in them.

The New Testament was written in the second half of the first century. It consists of 27 books written in Greek. Some of the books are brief that they are written in a page only. The first four books are called Gospels. The word gospel is derived from the old English word god spell meaning *good news*. Gospels contain the life and teaching of Jesus Christ.

The Bible has a central and significant place in the life and worship of a Christian church. The faith of Christianity is centered in Jesus Christ who is a historical person and who was born of a Jewish mother in Palestine whose earthly ended with his death on a cross on Good Friday but only to rise again with his resurrection on Easter Sunday. Jesus Christ is called the Lord who is everywhere.

The world is the realm of our earthly life and the world also signifies the arena of existence opposed to God. Man is fallen. His self-assertion is the root of Sin. Sin includes an individual and a cosmic dimension. God is related to the world in creations as well as redemption.

Man, according to Bible is made in the image and Likeness of God. He is a fallen creature and is redeemed by Jesus Christ. He is made a member of new humanity by Jesus Christ.

Educational Implications

Education is regarded as a significant activity in Christianity. Churches came forward to educate the masses by establishing schools in the beginning and universities later. Education to a Bible is a means to true moral life. An important aim of education is to enable the child to learn how to serve the individual as well as society. Christianity not only emphasizes the idea of social service but also tries to translate this idea into action by opening schools, hospitals and by training individuals to man them.

Aims of Education

Christian Education aims at brotherhood. Koinonia is a new Testament word used for followship. The human solidarity of forgiven sinners forms the source of a new type of community life and an important aim of education would be to enable the child to become a member of this community. One of the tasks of education is to make the individual understand the real purpose of sex and marriage.

The child has to know and practice Eucharist which means thanks giving. It was also called Lord's supper. It is a Christian act of worship now different forms of worship have developed. Liturgy is the name given to these forms. Originally it meant public service. Thus we can say that Christianity aims at multi-dimensional development of the personality of the child through education.

Curriculum

So far as curriculum is concerned Bible directs that individuals should have mastery over theology. Religion because an important part of Christian curriculum in the beginning but later on when church schools were established three R's viz., Reading, Writing and Arithmetic were emphasized. Thus language and mathematics were included in the curriculum as important subjects. Apart from Christian theology, Bible, three R's, ethics and some individual activities were included in the curriculum: E.g: helping the neighbours, serving the sufferers, nursing the patients in the hospital, treating the sick persons, preaching in the church, giving free education and teaching Bible in church and schools.

Method

Coming to method of teaching we can underline oral method since Bible contains oral sessions. Sometimes the ethical concepts are taught orally in the positive from and sometimes in the negative ones. Do not steal, do not be greedy are the examples of negative preaching and love they neighbour, obey they parents and elders are the examples of positive ones. Revelation may be cited as another method which has been indicated in the Bible. Psalm and proverbs are also used as devise in the Bible apart from letters which were aimed at giving divine messages. Later on self-learning, seminars, symposia, workshops, tutorials, monitorial system, activity oriented methods were also included in the methods of teaching in Christian schools. Christianity tries to develop modesty, humbleness, sincerity, honesty, dutifulness, obedience and simplicity in the students.

REFERENCES

1. Apple, M. (1979). *Ideology and Curriculum*. Boston: Routledge and Regan Paul.
2. Bowen, J. (1971). *A History of Western Education, Vol.2*. London: Methuen and Co.
3. Brameld, T. (1971). *Patterns of Educational Philosophy*. New York: Hold Rinehart and Winston.
4. Curtis, S. J. and Boultwood, M. (1953). *A Short History of Educational Ideas*. London: University Tutorial Press.

10

Jainism and Its Educational Implications

Jain Philosophy

In the Jain literature the term 'Jin' denotes one who has acquired perfect control over everything of a vicious nature or worldly pleasures of life. The preachings given by such conquerors over their senses constitute Jain religion.

Birth of Jainism

The founders of Jainism thought that the world was a place for various pleasures for most of the people. But when the population increased people abandoned the idea of enjoying the pleasures of life, because then they had to face various types of scarcities of life. So the ideal of enjoying pleasures was changed into performing work. Thus the world was then regarded as a place of work (Karma Bhumi). At this time fourteen Kulakars or Manus were born. These Men (Kulkars) developed traditions, conventions and customs for establishing a good social system. Because of such a developmental work these men were called Kulakars. (The one who works for the welfare of Kula or family was given the name Kulakar). In the Jain literature we find mention of only fourteen Kulakars. Of these fourteen, Nabhirai was the last Kulakar. Nabhirai had a son named Rikhabhadev. Rikhabhadev is considered to be the first propounder of Jainism. In fact, Jainism developed from him. In the Jain literature Lord Rikhabhadev is regarded as 'Jin' (the conqueror of all senses) or Tirthankar. Jainism is a collection of preaching of such twenty-four Tirthankars of who Lord Rikhabhadev was the first and Lord Mahavir was the last, Lord Mahavir was born in 800 B.C. in a village named Kundagram. His father's name was Siddharth. Trishal was his mother. The Viashali area of Bihar is regarded as his birth place. Lord Mahavir would not stand the slaughtering of innocent animals in Yajan (Yagya). At the age of 30, he became disillusioned with the world and he performed hard penance for twelve years. As a result, he got light of knowledge (Gyanjyati). After this for thirty years he preached his religion known as Jainism. He obtained salvation (Nirvan) at the age of 72 years.

Principles of Jain Philosophy

According to Jain Philosophy there are three main elements in each matter - (1) Ulpad, (2) Vyay and (3) Dhraubya. These three principal elements are respectively indicative of (1) Ulpati, i.e., birth, origin or creation, (2) Vinash, i.e., destruction or annihilation and (3) Sthirat. i.e., stability. The process of birth and destruction of these elements never stops. It is on this basis that Jain philosophy regards this world as changeable. But in spite of this changeability the unity of the world is maintained in the same way as a man changes from infancy to adolescence, adulthood and old age, but his unity as a man is maintained. On this basis the Jain religion believes that unchangeability is always continued along with changes.

According to Jainism this worked is eternal and endless. Jains believe that this world is not made by anyone. The world is made of Jiva, i.e., spirit and Ajiva, i.e., matter (which is lifeless and inanimate). The Ajiva or the matter is or five types-Pudgai, Dharma, Adharma, Akash and Kai. These five elements always remain constant. Neither they decrease nor increase. Jainism does not believe in the existence of God. Neither God creates nor destroys, simply because is (i.e., God's) very concept is baseless.

Antheism (or Anishwarvad) of Jainism

As already referred to above. Jainism does not believe in the existence of God. The propounders of Jainism regard the concept of God as irrelevant. They contend that in order to prove the truthfulness of any so-called truth, "there should be some proof", then God is not cognizable and he is out of the purview of our senses.

Jainism sees the same thing into different forms. According to this philosophy a 'truth' (Satya) may be seen with varying viewpoints. Therefore a true Jain does not stick to a particular point of view, not does he insist on his own views in the process of reasoning. He has a liberal outlook. He believes that a particular thing may be perceived in different ways. Because of this attitude a true Jain is able to maintain a Sambhav or poise or equilibrium in face of all circumstances. This attitude is known as Syadvad.

The Educational Implications of the Principle of Anekantvad

Anekantvad implies liberalism. This principle classifies that only one aspect of a thing or issue cannot be acceptable. Regarding or proposition there may be two or more sides. Therefore, in order to reach a right judgement on a certain issue, we have to take into consideration its various aspects. In the democratic era of these days it is quite natural to have various points of view regarding a certain idea. It is not possible that the stand of a teacher or that of any student in a class will be accepted by all the students, in the classes. Therefore, it is necessary to effect a co-ordination between the various views expressed by students in a class. In reaching a decision each student should have the self-satisfaction that his viewpoints have also been duty considered and the same have been accommodated in the final deliberation. This feeling on the part of the student will promote the development of his personality and will help in adopting a liberal attitude about things. On the class teaching of modern days the teacher should try to co-ordinate the various views of the students for posing a consistent whole. Evidently, the same idea must not be imposed on all students.

Non-Violence

Non-violence is the main basis of Jainism. In fact, it is its main philosophy of behaviour. Non-violence has been given the highest place in the life of a follower of Jainism. Violence against any inanimate or animate being is strictly prohibited in Jainism. We are very much prone to commit violence in our various simple and complex activities. Jainism enjoins that everyone should always try to avoid any kind of violence. We must not commit violence in any situation. Even to hurt anyone's feelings is a kind of violence. It is well known that because of fear of committing violence, a follower of Jainism does not take food in the night. He keeps his lips and nostrils wrapped up with thin pieces of cloth in order to prevent entering of germs into the body through them.

Educational Implications of Non-Violence

Today the entire world is besieged with various of violence. One country wants to establish its supremacy over another through hurting its feelings. In some part of the world some battle is being fought between two countries. Extremists and terrorists are having their sway all over the world.

The Theory of Karma (The Bondage of the Being)

In Jainism the relationship between 'being' (the animate) and the inanimate (Jadm Pudgal or the body matter) has been regarded as a bondage. In Jainism the animate, the being or the 'Jiva' has been accepted as the consciousness (Chetan). The animate epitomizes unlimited knowledge (Anant Gyan), unlimited vision (Anant Darshan) unlimited prowess (Valour or Ananat Virya) and unlimited enjoyment (Bliss or Anant Anand). As a result of its deeds (Karma), ignorance (Agyanta), envelops the being (Jiva) and all these powers vanish and the 'being' (Jiva) is encircled into a bondage. If the Jiva (the being) acquires knowledge, he will recapture all these powers and obtain salvation and his form will becomes full of lustres. Here a relevant matter (Ajiva) Jainism believes that this association or bondage comes through Karmas (or deeds). Because of his bondage the one influence the other (i.e., the Jiva (being), it reacts on the Pudgal i.e., the body matter) and the forms of the two are changes. Because of attachments (Raga) and Malice (Dvesha) the Jiva happens to perform various deeds. A certain matter (property-Dravya) enter into the being as a result of his mental and physical activities. Consequently, the Jiva gets into a bondage.

Jainism believes that whatever the Jiva (the Being animate) gets is a result of his deeds. The colour, form of the body, age and the various senses are the results of one's deeds. This analysis of Karma is a special aspect of Jain philosophy. Jainism does not believe that God is the determiner of one's fate or destiny. In fact, Jainism does not believe in the existence of God. Whatever man gets in his life is a result of his deeds and not a kindness of God (Ishwar Kripa). The man is the maker of his 'good' or 'bad'. No unseen power influences the Jiva.

Educational Implication of the Concept of Salvation According to Jainism

Now it is not difficult to understand the educational ideas implies in the concept of salvation according to Jainism. In a way, it will not be an exaggeration to say that the ultimate purpose of education is attainment of salvation. In this sense, salvation (Moksha) and education become synonymous. If we have not attachment with worldly things our various types of drives will vanish. Then we shall be oriented towards attainment of perfection or salvation. As a result, all our activities will be directed towards seeking welfare of others. The various tools for attainment of salvation, as prescribed by Jainism may be regarded as tools for achieving ideals of education also.

REFERENCES

1. Mohanty, J. *Indian Education in the Emerging Society*, New Delhi, 1982.
2. Radhakrishnan, S. & Moore. *Source Book of Indian Philosophy*. Allen and Uncoin.
3. Rena, R. *Introduction to Indian Philosophy*. New Delhi: Tala Mac Graw Hill, 1971.
4. Rusk R. Robert. *A History of Indian Education*. London: University of London Press, 1951.
5. Sharma, Ram Nath (2000). *Text Book of Educational Philosophy*. New Delhi: Kanishka Publishers, Distributors.
6. Vivekananda. *Complete Works of Swami Vivekananda*. Advits Publishers, Vol. V, 1982.

11
Perennialism and Essentialism

Perennialism is a theory of education that draws heavily on the principles of Realism. Like realism and idealism also, Perennialism, as its name implies, represents a conservative or a traditional view of education. It is based on the belief that human nature is constant and that the basic principles of education are changeless and recurrent. Emphasizing the intellectual character of both the person and the universe, Perennialists accept Aristotle's statement that man is a rational animal. For them the school is a social agency designed to cultivate human intelligence.

The Perennialists see the universal aim of education as the search for and the dissemination of truth. Truth is universal and unchanging; hence, a genuine education is also universal and constant. The school's curriculum should emphasize the universal and recurrent themes of human life. It should contain cognitive subjects that cultivate rationality and the study of moral, aesthetic and religious principles to cultivate the attitudinal dimension. Like the idealists and realists, the Perennialists prefer a subject-matter curriculum. The Perennialist curriculum includes history, language, mathematics, logic, literature the humanities and science.

Hutchins has long argued that education ought to cultivate the intellect along with the harmonious development of all human faculties. The central aim of education should be the development of the power of thought. Whereas most educators justify the emphasis on thought because it organizes and enriches life experiences, Hutchins derives it from a definition of the fixed and essential nature of human beings. Hutchins has described the ideal education as

> ... one that develops intellectual power I arrive at this conclusion by a process of elimination. Educational institution are the only institutions that can develop intellectual power. The ideal education is not an adhoc education, not an education directed to immediate needs; it is not a specialized education, or a pre-professional education; it is not a utilitarian education. It is an education calculated to develop the mind.

Hutchins bases his educational philosophy on two major premises: human nature is rational and knowledge resides in unchanging, absolute and universal truths. Since the rationality of human nature is universal, Hutchins stresses that education must also be universal. Since reason is our highest power, the development of the intellect should be education's highest priority. Hutchins advocates a curriculum that consists of permanent or perennial studies. He particularly recommends the study of the classics or the great works of western civilization. Reading and discussing great books will cultivate the intellect and will prepare students to think carefully and critically. In addition to these classics, he urges the study of grammer, rhetoric, logic, mathematics and philosophy.

In general, perennialism represents a conservative theoretical position centered on the authority of tradition and the classic. Among its major educational principles are:

1. Truth is universal and does not depend on the circumstances of places, time or persons.
2. A good education involves a search for and an understanding of the truth.
3. Education is a liberal exercise that develops the intellect.

ESSENTIALISM

Essentialism is a conservative educational theory that arose as a response to progressive education. Essentialism is basically a position that emphasize the authority of the teacher and the value of the subject-matter curriculum. For the essentialists education involves the learning of the basic skills, arts and sciences that have been developed in the past. These essential skills-reading, writing, and arithmetic—are to be found in every sound elementary school curriculum. At the secondary level the basic curriculum consists of history, mathematics, science, language and literature. Mastering these skills and subjects prepares the student to function as a member of a civilized society. In addition, the student also should acquire the behaviour that is needed for successful living. The learning of the essential curriculum requires discipline and hard work. Those who aspire to be teaching should be skilled professionals both in subject matter and in teaching.

Arthur Bestor, an advocate of contemporary essentialism, sees the liberal arts and sciences as the core of a general education that will enable all men and women to function intelligently. Bestor and the members of the Conservative Council on Basic Education have argued that the intellectual quality of American education has been weakened by those professional educators who have stressed life adjustment and other non-essentials.

Essentialists hold that these intellectual disciplines should be basic in the school curriculum since they are necessary foundations of modern life. In the elementary school curriculum, reading, writing, arithmetic and research skills are the indispensable studies. The high school curriculum should consists of science, mathematics, history, english and foreign language. These are the tools of a liberal education and the most reliable aids in meeting the requirements of both personal and social life. It is the task of the school to channel the accumulated experience of humankind into the organized coherent and differentiated disciplines. Only after mastering these basic disciplines can the student be expected to use them to solve personal, social and civic problems.

Certain common themes can be found in the essentialist position. Among them are:

1. The elementary school curriculum should aim to cultivate basic tool skills that contribute to literacy and mastery of arithmetical computation.
2. The secondary curriculum should cultivate competencies in history, mathematics, science, literature, english and foreign languages.
3. Schooling requires discipline and a respect or legitimate authority.
4. Learning requires hard work and disciplined attention.

REFERENCES

1. Belock & Green J.L. (Ed.). *Philosophy and Education.* Meerut: Any Prakashan.
2. Brubacher, J.S. (Ed.) (1955). *Philosophies of Education.* Chicago: University of Chicago Press.
3. Butler—*Four Philosophies of Education.*
4. Hocking. W.E. (1938). *Types of Philosophy.* New York: Charles Scribuses Sons.
5. Martin W.O. (1969). *Realism in Education.* New York: Harper & Row.
6. Reid, L.A. (1962). *Philosophy and Education.* London: Heinsmann.

12
Realism

Realism stresses objective knowledge and values as does idealism, but the realist view of metaphysics and epistemology is different. A basic definition describes the three basic doctrines of realism as follows:

1. There is a world of real existence which human beings have not made or constructed.
2. This real existence can be known by the human mind.
3. Such knowledge is the only reliable guide to human conduct, individual and social.

This definition provides a convenient starting point for considering the educational implications of Realist metaphysics, epistemology and axiology.

Metaphysics and epistemology to the Realist there is a material world that exists independently and externally to the mind of the knower. The basis for understanding reality is found in a world of objects and in the perceptions of these objects. All objects are composed of matter. Matter must be encased in a form and has to assume the structure of a particular object.

Human beings can know these objects through their senses and their reason. Knowing is a process that involves two stages: sensation and abstraction. First, the knower sees an object and records the sensory data about it such as colour, size, weight, smell or sound. These sensory data are sorted out in the mind into those qualities that are always present in the object and those qualities that are sometimes present in the object. Upon the abstraction of the necessary qualities of an object the learner comes to a concept of the object. Conceptualization results when the mind has abstracted the form of an object and has recognized the object as belonging to a class. Objects are classified when they are recognized as having qualities that they share with other members of the same class but not with objects that belong to a different class.

The realist theory of knowledge has also been referred to as a "spectator theory." This simply means that men and women are spectators or onlookers in the world. In their experience people see many objects. Some of them are two-legged creatures like themselves, others are four-legged or other forms of the animal kingdom and still other objects are plants or minerals. As spectators of reality, men and women engage in a process of sorting out these objects according to their form or structure. They classify those objects that are alike into related classifications. Again as spectators their conception of an object is accurate when it corresponds with the structure of an object in reality.

Like the idealist, the realist believes that a curriculum consisting of organized, separate subject matters is the most effective and efficient way of learning about the reality of the objective order. Organizing subject matter, as scientists and scholars do, is simply a sophisticated method of classifying objects. For example, the past experiences of human kind can be organized into history. Plants can be studied in a systematic way according to their classifications in the subject matter of botany. Animals can be studied in the subject of zoology. Units of political organization such as nations, governments, legislatures and judicial systems can be organized into the study of political science. For the realist the way to gain knowledge of reality is to pursue ordered and disciplined inquiry through these compartmentalized bodies of knowledge or subject matters.

Axiology

Based upon the Realist's conception of knowledge, certain prescriptions can be identified to govern intelligent behaviour. For example, human beings out to be have in a rational way; behaviour is rational when it conforms to the way in which objects behave in reality. From their study of the subjects that explain reality, men and women can arrive at theories that are based on natural physical and social laws. The rational person governs his or her behaviour in the light of such tested theory.

REFERENCES

1. Belock & Green J.L. (Ed.). *Philosophy and Education*. Meerut: Any Prakashan.
2. Brubacher, J.S. (Ed.) (1955). *Philosophies of Education*. Chicago: University of Chicago Press.
3. Butler—*Four Philosophies of Education*.
4. Hocking. W.E. (1938). *Types of Philosophy*. New York: Charles Scribuses Sons.
5. Martin W.O. (1969). *Realism in Education*. New York: Harper & Row.
6. Reid, L.A. (1962). *Philosophy and Education*. London: Heinsmann.

13
Great Indian Educators

SWAMI VIVEKANANDA

Life Sketch

Swami Vivekananda (January 12, 1863–July 4, 1902), born Narendranath Dutta is the chief disciple of the 19th century mystic Ramakrishna and the founder of Ramakrishna Mission. He is considered a key figure in the introduction of Vedanta and Yoga in Europe and America and is also credited with raising interfaith awareness, bringing Hinduism to the status of a world religion during the end of the 19th Century. Vivekananda is considered to be a major force in the revival of Hinduism in modern India. He is best known for his inspiring speech beginning with "sisters and brothers of America",through which he introduced Hinduism at the Parliament of the World's Religions at Chicago in 1893.

Swami Vivekananda was born in an aristocratic family of Calcutta in 1863. His parents influenced the Swami's thinking-the father by his rational mind and the mother by her religious temperament. From his childhood, he showed inclination towards spirituality and God realization. While searching for a man who could directly demonstrate the reality of God, he came to Ramakrishna and became his disciple. As a Guru Ramakrishna taught him Advaita Vedanta and that all religions are true and service to man was the most effective worship of God. After the death of his Guru, he became a wandering monk touring the Indian subcontinent and getting a first hand account of India's condition. He later sailed to Chicago and represented India as a delegate in the 1893 Parliament of World religions. An eloquent speaker, Vivekananda was invited to several forums in United States and spoke at universities and clubs. He conducted several public and private lectures, disseminating Vedanta, Yoga and Hinduism in America, England and few other countries in Europe. He also established Vedanta societies in America and England. He later sailed back to India and in 1897 he founded the Ramakrishna Math and Mission, a philanthropic and spiritual organization. The Swami is regarded as one of India's foremost nation-builders. His teachings influenced the thinking of other national leaders and philosophers, like Mahatma Gandhi, Jawaharlal Nehru, Subhash Chandra Bose, Aurobindo Ghosh, Radhakrishnan.

Philosophy

Vivekananda was a renowned thinker in his own right. One of his most important contributions was to demonstrate how Advaitin thinking is not merely philosophically far-reaching, but how it also has social, even political, consequences. According to Vivekananda, a important lesson he received from Ramakrishna was that "Jiva is Shiva" (each individual is divinity itself). This became his Mantra, and he coined the concept of *daridra narayana seva*—the service of God in and through (poor) human beings. If there truly is the unity of Brahman underlying all phenomena, then on what basis do we regard ourselves as better or worse or even as better-off or worse-off, than others?—This was the question he posed to himself. Ultimately, he concluded that these distinctions fade into nothingness in the light of the oneness that the devotee experiences in *Moksha.* What arises then is compassion for those "individuals" who remain unaware of this oneness and a determination to help them.

Swami Vivekananda belonged to that branch of Vedanta that held that no one can be truly free until all of us are. Even the desire for personal salvation has to be given up and only tireless work for the salvation of others is the true mark of the enlightened person. He founded the Sri Ramakrishna Math and Mission on the principle of *Atmano Mokshartham Jagat-hitaya cha* (for one's own salvation and for the welfare of the World).

However, Vivekananda also pleaded for a strict separation between religion and government ("church and state") a value found in Freemasonry which as a Freemason he had been exposed to.

Although social customs had been formed in the past with religious sanction, it was not now the business of religion to interfere with matters such as marriage, inheritance and so on. The ideal society would be a mixture of Brahmin knowledge, Kshatriya culture, Vaisya efficiency and the egalitarian Shudra ethos. Domination by any one led to different sorts of lopsided societies. Vivekananda did not feel that religion, nor, any force for that matter, should be used forcefully to bring about an ideal society, since this was something that would evolve naturally by individualistic change when the conditions were right.

Vivekananda made a strict demarcation between the two classes of Hindu scriptures: the Sruti and the Smritis. The Sruti, by which is meant the Vedas, consist of eternally and universally valid spiritual truths. The Smritis on the other hand, are the dos and donts of religions, applicable to society and subject to revision from time to time. Vivekananda felt that existing Hindu Smritis had to be revised for modern times. But the Srutis of course are eternal - they may only be re-interpreted.

Vivekananda advised his followers to be holy, unselfish and have Shraddha (faith). He encouraged the practice of Brahmacharya (Celibacy). In one of the conversations with his childhood friend Priya Nath Sinha he attributes his physical and mental strengths, eloquence to the practice of Brahmacharya.

Vivekananda didn't advocate the emerging area of parapsychology, astrology (one instance can be found in his speech Man the Maker of his Destiny, Complete-Works, Volume 8, Notes of Class Talks and Lectures) saying that this form of curiosity doesn't help in spiritual progress but actually hinders it.

Educational Philosophy

Vivekananda defines education as, "the manifestation of perfection already in man." He believes in auto education or self teaching. As is the plant, so is the child. The growth and development of a plant and that of a child takes place according to their nature. A gardener prepares the ground for the growth of his plants, protects them and nurrishes them so that they grow properly. Similarly, the teacher takes care of the child, provides him a suitable environment and looks after his proper growth. Thus though education comes from within, the teacher is an indispensable part of it. While the motivation comes from within, the teacher activates it. He encourages the child to use his mind, body and sense organs properly and achieve maximum development.

Main Publications

Vivekananda left a body of philosophical works which Vedic scholar Frank Parlato has called, "the greatest comprehensive work in philosophy ever published." His books (compiled from lectures given around the world) on the four Yogas (Raja Yoga, Karma Yoga, Bhakti Yoga, Jnana Yoga) are very influential and still seen as fundamental texts for anyone interested in the Hindu practice of Yoga. His letters are of great literary and spiritual value. He was also considered a very good singer and a poet. By he had composed many songs including his favourite Kali the Mother.

RABINDRANATH TAGORE

Life Sketch

Rabindranath Tagore (7 May 1861 - 7 August 1941), also known by the sobriquet Gurudev, was a Bengali poet, visual artist, playwright, novelist and composer whose works reshaped Bengali literature and music in the late 19th and early 20th centuries. He became Asia's first Nobel laureate when he won the 1913 Nobel Prize in Literature.

Tagore wrote novels, short stories, songs, dance-dramas and essays on political and personal topics. Gitanjali (Song Offerings), Gora (Fair-Faced) and Ghare-Baire (The Home and the World) are among his best-known works. His verse, short stories and novels, which often exhibited rhythmic lyricism, colloquial language, meditative naturalism and philosophical contemplation, received worldwide acclaim. Tagore was also a cultural reformer and polymath who modernised Bengali art by rejecting strictures binding it to classical Indian forms. Two songs from his canon are now the national anthems of Bangladesh and India: the Amar Shonar Bangla and the Jana Gana Mana respectively.

Tagore (nicknamed "Rabi") was born the youngest of thirteen surviving children in the Jorasanko mansion in Calcutta (now Kolkata, India) of parents Debendranath Tagore (1817-1905) and Sarada Devi (1830-1875). The Tagore family were the Brahmo founding fathers of the Adi Dharm faith. After undergoing his upanayan at age eleven, Tagore and his father left Calcutta on 14 February 1873 to tour India for several months, visiting his father's Santiniketan estate and Amritsar before reaching the Himalayan hill station of Dalhousie. There, Tagore read biographies, studied history, astronomy, modern science and Sanskrit and examined the classical poetry of Kālidāsa.

Seeking to become a barrister, Tagore enrolled at a public school in Brighton, England in 1878. He studied law at University College London, but returned to Bengal in 1880 without a degree. On 9 December 1883 he married Mrinalini Devi.

In 1901, Tagore left Shilaidaha and moved to Santiniketan (West Bengal) to found an ashram, which would grow to include a marble-floored prayer hall, an experimental school, groves of trees, gardens and a library. There, Tagore's wife and two of his children died. His father died on 19 January 1905, and he began receiving monthly payments as part of his inheritance. On 14 November 1913, Tagore learned that he had won the 1913 Nobel Prize in Literature. According to the Swedish Academy, it was given due to the idealistic and—for Western readers—accessible nature of a small body of his translated material, including the 1912 Gitanjali: Song Offerings. In 1915, Tagore received the knighthood from the British Crown. But as a mark of rebuke to the rulers, post the Jallianwala Bagh massacre in 1919, he renounced the title.

In 1921, Tagore and agricultural economist Leonard Knight Elmhirst set up the Institute for Rural Reconstruction (which Tagore later renamed Shriniketan—"Abode of Wealth") in Surul, a village near the ashram at Santiniketan. Through it, Tagore sought to provide an alternative to Gandhi's symbol—and protest-based Swaraj movement, which he denounced. He recruited scholars, donors and officials from many countries to help the Institute use schooling to "free village[s] from the shackles of helplessness and ignorance" by "vitaliz[ing] knowledge." In the early 1930s, he also grew more concerned about India's "abnormal caste consciousness" and untouchability, lecturing on its evils, writing poems and dramas with untouchable protagonists and appealing to authorities at the Guruvayoor Temple to admit Dalits.

Tagore's last four years were marked by chronic pain and two long periods of illness. These began when Tagore lost consciousness in late 1937; he remained comatose and near death for an extended period. This was followed three years later in late 1940 by a similar spell, from which he never recovered. The poetry Tagore wrote in these years is among his finest and is distinctive for its preoccupation with death. After extended suffering, Tagore died on 7 August 1941 (22 Shravan 1348) in an upstairs room of the Jorasanko mansion in which he was raised; his death anniversary is still mourned in public functions held across the Bengali-speaking world.

Philosophy

Tagore believed in the vedas. He was of the view that God is one and he is the creator of man as well as of nature. He believed that in him and through him we find unity between man and man and unity between man and nature.

Educational Philosophy

Tagore's educational philosophy has been drawn from his philosophy of life. Freedom, creative self-expression and active communication with nature and man are three cardinal principles of his educational philosophy. According to him there are three sources of knowledge. They are nature, life and the teacher.

Main Publications

His main publications were more in the field of poetry and literature, but he contributed a few essays on education as well. *Gitanjali, My school, Sadhana, Greater India, The gardener, Creative unity, Personality, Fruit gathering* etc. are a few among them.

MAHATMA GANDHI

Life Sketch

Mohandas Karamchand Gandhi (2 October 1869 – 30 January 1948) was a major political and spiritual leader of India and the Indian independence movement. He was the pioneer of satyagraha—resistance to tyranny through mass civil disobedience, firmly founded upon ahimsa or total non-violence-which led India to independence and inspired movements for civil rights and freedom across the world. He is commonly known around the world as Mahatma Gandhi an honorific first applied to him by Rabindranath Tagore and in India also as Bapu. He is officially honoured in India as the Father of the Nation; his birthday, 2 October, is commemorated there as Gandhi Jayanti, a national holiday and worldwide as the International Day of Non-Violence.

Gandhi first employed non-violent civil disobedience as an expatriate lawyer in South Africa, in the resident Indian community's struggle for civil rights. After his return to India in 1915, he set about organising peasants, farmers and urban labourers in protesting excessive land-tax and discrimination. Assuming leadership of the Indian National Congress in 1921, Gandhi led nationwide campaigns for easing poverty, expanding women's rights, building religious and ethnic amity, ending untouchability, increasing economic self-reliance, but above all achieving Swaraj—the independence of India from foreign domination. Gandhi famously led Indians in the Non-cooperation movement in 1922 and in protesting the British-imposed salt tax with the 400 km. Dandi Salt March in 1930 and later in calling for the British to Quit India in 1942. He was imprisoned for many years, on numerous occasions, in both South Africa and India.

As a practitioner of Ahimsa Gandhi swore to speak the truth, and advocated that others do the same. He lived modestly in a self-sufficient residential community and wore the traditional Indian dhoti and shawl, woven with yarn he had hand spun on a charkha. He ate simple vegetarian food and also undertook long fasts as means of both self-purification and social protest.

Mohandas Karamchand Gandhi was born in Porbander, a coastal town in present-day Gujarat, India, on 2 October 1869. His father, Karamchand Gandhi (1822-1885), who belonged to the Hindu Modh community, was the diwan (Prime Minister) of the eponymous Porbander state, a small princely state in the Kathiawar Agency of British India. His mother, Putlibai, who came from the Hindu Pranami Vaishnava community, was Karamchand's fourth wife, the first three wives having apparently died in childbirth. Growing up with a devout mother and the Jain traditions of the region, the young Mohandas absorbed early the influences that would play an important role in his adult life; these included compassion to sentient beings, vegetarianism, fasting for self-purification and mutual tolerance between individuals of different creeds.

In May 1883, the 13-year old Mohandas was married to 14-year old Kasturbai Makhanji (her first name was usually shortened to

"Kasturba," and affectionately to "Ba") in an arranged child marriage, as was the custom in the region However, as was also the custom of the region, the adolescent bride was to spend much time at her parents' house and away from her husband. In 1885, when Gandhi was 15, the couple's first child was born, but survived only a few days; Gandhi's father, Karamchand Gandhi, had died earlier that year. Mohandas and Kasturbai had four more children, all sons: Harilal, born in 1888; Manilal, born in 1892; Ramdas, born in 1897; and Devdas, born in 1900. At his middle school in Porbandar and high school in Rajkot, Gandhi remained an average student academically. He passed the matriculation exam for Samaldas College at Bhavnagar, Gujarat with some difficulty. While there, he was unhappy, in part because his family wanted him to become a barrister.

On 4 September 1888, less than a month shy of his nineteenth birthday, Gandhi travelled to London, England, to study law at University College London and to train as a barrister. His time in London, the Imperial capital, was influenced by a vow he had made to his mother in the presence of the Jain monk Becharji, upon leaving India, to observe the Hindu precepts of abstinence from meat, alcohol, and promiscuity. Although Gandhi experimented with adopting "English" customs—taking dancing lessons for example—he could not stomach his landlady's mutton and cabbage. She pointed him towards one of London's few vegetarian restaurants. Rather than simply go along with his mother's wishes, he read about, and intellectually embraced vegetarianism. He joined the Vegetarian Society, was elected to its executive committee, and founded a local chapter. He later credited this with giving him valuable experience in organizing institutions. Some of the vegetarians he met were members of the Theosophical Society, which had been founded in 1875 to further universal brotherhood, and which was devoted to the study of Buddhist and Hindu literature. They encouraged Gandhi to read the Bhagavad Gita. Not having shown a particular interest in religion before, he read works of and about Hinduism, Christianity, Buddhism, Islam and other religions. He returned to India after being called to the bar of England and Wales by the Inner Temple but had limited success establishing a law practice in Mumbai. Later, after applying and being turned down for a part-time job as a high school teacher, he ended up returning to Rajkot to make a modest living drafting petitions for litigants, a business he was forced to close when he ran afoul of a British officer. In his autobiography, he refers to this incident as an unsuccessful attempt to lobby on behalf of his older brother. It was in this climate that, in 1893, he accepted a year-long contract from an Indian firm to a post in Natal, South Africa, then part of the British Empire.

Philosophy

Truth: Gandhi dedicated his life to the wider purpose of discovering truth or Satya. He tried to achieve this by learning from his own mistakes and conducting experiments on himself. He called his autobiography *The Story of My Experiments with Truth*.

Gandhi stated that the most important battle to fight was overcoming his own demons, fears and insecurities. Gandhi summarized his beliefs first when he said "God is Truth." He would later change this statement to "Truth is God." Thus, Satya (Truth) in Gandhi's philosophy is "God."

Non-violence: Although Mahatama Gandhi was in no way the originator of the principle of non-violence, he was the first to apply it in the political field on a huge scale. The concept of non-violence (ahimsa) and non-resistance has a long history in Indian religious thought and has had many revivals in Hindu, Buddhist, Jain, Jewish and Christian contexts. Gandhi explains his philosophy and way of life in his autobiography The Story of My Experiments with Truth. He was quoted as saying:

Vegetarianism: As a young child, Gandhi experimented with meat-eating. This was due partially to his inherent curiosity as well as his rather persuasive peer and friend Sheikh Mehtab. The idea of vegetarianism is deeply ingrained in Hindu and Jain traditions in India, and, in his native land of Gujarat, most Hindus were vegetarian and so are almost all Jains. The Gandhi family was no exception. Before leaving for his studies in London, Gandhi made a promise to his mother, Putlibai and his uncle, Becharji Swami that he would abstain from eating meat, taking alcohol, and engaging in promiscuity. He held fast to his promise and gained more than a diet: he gained a basis for his life-long philosophies. As Gandhi grew into adulthood, he became a strict vegetarian. He wrote the book The Moral Basis of Vegetarianism and several articles on the subject, some of which were published in the London Vegetarian Society's publication, The Vegetarian. During this period, the young

Gandhi became inspired by many great minds and was befriended by the Chairman of the London Vegetarian Society, Dr. Josiah Oldfield.

Brahmacharya: When Gandhi was 16 his father became very ill. Being very devoted to his parents, he attended to his father at all times during his illness. However, one night, Gandhi's uncle came to relieve Gandhi for a while. He retired to his bedroom where carnal desires overcame him and he made love to his wife. Shortly afterward a servant came to report that Gandhi's father had just died. Gandhi felt tremendous guilt and never could forgive himself. He came to refer to this event as "double shame." The incident had significant influence in Gandhi becoming celibate at the age of 36, while still married.

Simplicity: Gandhi earnestly believed that a person involved in social service should lead a simple life which he thought could lead to Brahmacharya. His simplicity began by renouncing the western lifestyle he was leading in South Africa. He called it "reducing himself to zero," which entailed giving up unnecessary expenditure, embracing a simple lifestyle and washing his own clothes. On one occasion he returned the gifts bestowed to him from the natals for his diligent service to the community.

Gandhi spent one day of each week in silence. He believed that abstaining from speaking brought him inner peace. This influence was drawn from the Hindu principles of mauna (silence) and shanti (peace). On such days he communicated with others by writing on paper. For three and a half years, from the age of 37, Gandhi refused to read newspapers, claiming that the tumultuous state of world affairs caused him more confusion than his own inner unrest.

Faith: Gandhi was born a Hindu and practised Hinduism all his life, deriving most of his principles from Hinduism. As a common Hindu, he believed all religions to be equal and rejected all efforts to convert him to a different faith. He was an avid theologian and read extensively about all major religions.

Educational Philosophy

Mahatma Gandhi's contribution to the field of educational theory and practice is really outstanding. He has been consider to be a revolutionary educational thinker of modern India. Through his educational scheme usually known as basic education he wanted to bring about a social revolution in our country, that would result in creation of a new social order, that would reflect his philosophy of education and life. Gandhiji was at the same time an idealist, a naturalist, a pragmatist and a humanist.

Main Publications

Gandhi was a prolific writer. For decades he edited several newspapers including *Harijan* in Gujarati, Hindi and English; *Indian Opinion* while in South Africa and, *Young India,* in English and *Navajivan,* a Gujarati monthly, on his return to India. Later *Navajivan* was also published in Hindi. In addition, he wrote letters almost every day to individuals and newspapers.

Gandhi also wrote a few books including his autobiography, An Autobiography of *My Experiments with Truth, Satyagraha* in South Africa about his struggle there, *Hind Swaraj* or *Indian Home Rule,* a political pamphlet and a paraphrase in Gujarati of John Ruskin's Unto This Last. This last essay can be considered his programme on economics. He also wrote extensively on vegetarianism, diet and health, religion, social reforms, etc. Gandhi usually wrote in Gujarati, though he also revised the Hindi and English translations of his books.

Gandhi's complete works were published by the Indian government under the name The Collected Works of Mahatma Gandhi in the 1960s. The writings comprise about 50,000 pages published in about a hundred volumes. In 2000, a revised edition of the complete works sparked a controversy, as Gandhian followers argue that the government incorporated the changes for political purposes. The Indian government later withdrew the revised edition.

SRI AUROBINDO GHOSH

Life Sketch

Sri Aurobindo (August 15, 1872–December 5, 1950) was an Indian nationalist, scholar, poet, mystic, evolutionary philosopher, Yogi and spiritual master. After a short political career in which he became one of the leaders of the early movement for Indian independence from British rule, Sri Aurobindo turned to the exploration of the subtle realms of human existence and as a consequence, developed a his own vision and philosophy of human progress and a spiritual path which he termed Integral Yoga.

The central theme of Sri Aurobindo's vision is the evolution of life into a "life divine." Pronounced and often written as "Ghosh" (or "Arabindo Ghosh"), in Kolkata (Calcutta), India, on 15th August, 1872. Aravind means Lotus (pronounced "Aurobindo" in Bengali). His father was Dr. K.D. Ghose and his mother Swarnalata Devi.

Dr. Ghose (who had lived in Britain and studied medicine at Aberdeen University), was determined that his children should have an English education and upbringing free of any Indian influences. He therefore sent the young Aurobindo and his siblings to the Loreto Convent school in Darjeeling. Subsequently, at the age of seven, Aurobindo was taken (along with his two elder brothers Manmohan and Benoybhusan) to Manchester, England and placed in the care of a Mr. and Mrs. Drewett-an Anglican clergyman and his wife-who tutored Aurobindo privately. Mr. Drewett, himself a capable scholar, grounded Aurobindo so well in Latin that Aurobindo was able to gain admission into St. Paul's School in London. At St. Paul's Aurobindo learned Greek and Latin. The last three years at St. Paul's were spent in reading literature, especially English Poetry. At St. Paul's he received the Butterworth Prize for literature, the Bedford Prize for history and a scholarship to King's College, Cambridge University. He returned to India in 1893.

Philosophy

Sri Aurobindo argues that humankind as an entity is not the last rung in the evolutionary scale, but can evolve spiritually beyond its current limitations associated with an essential ignorance to a future state of supramental existence. This further evolutionary step would lead to a divine life on Earth characterized by a supramental or truth-consciousness and a transformed and divinised life and material form.

Educational Philosophy

Aurobindo's educational system can be summed up in to two words 'Integral Education'. This system has two functions to serve.

1. It gives an integrated view of the universe to the pupil.
2. Education attempts at an all-round balanced harmonious and integrated development of the individual.

Main Publications

The Life Divine, The Synthesis of Yoga, Essays on The Gita, The Secret of

The Veda, Hymns to the Mystic Fire, The Upanishads, The Foundations of Indian Culture, War and Self-determination, The Human Cycle, The Ideal of Human Unity, and *The Future Poetry, Renaissance in India on Education, A System of National Education,* etc. are his famous books.

MAULANA ABUL KALAM AZAD- The Builder of Modern India

Maulana Abul Kalam Azad (11 November 1888- 22 February 1958) a striking personality among the ranks of Muslim thinkers and political activists advocating Indian nationalism based on the unity of all religio-ethnic communities. An outstanding politician of the Gandhian School and first Education Minister of India, Abul Kalam Ghulam Muhiyuddin (pen name Azad) was born in Mecca. His mother was an Arab and his father, Maulana Khairuddin, was a Bengal Muslim of Afghan origins. Khairuddin left India during the Sepoy Revolt an proceeded to Mecca and settled there. He came back Kolkata with his family in 1890.

Abul Kalam Azad was one of those geniuses whose names are written with golden letters in the pages of history. All of them contributed their energies in various ways. They not only structured the syllabi but also formulated the policies in order to carry the light of education in the remotest rural areas. They also chalked out programmes for the training of teachers to make them abreast of the developments taking place in the world of education.

The 'National Education Day' (11th November) is of course a day to pledge to work on various initiatives taken under the Sarva Shiksha Abhiyan (SSA) in setting up model schools in secondary education; on the various initiatives takes in higher secondary education: and in vocational and higher education sectors by the Central Government on its own; and in partnership with State Governments, as well as through private public partnership for the re-organization of present system of education in the country.

The questions remains which, the educational strata has to answer. Have we as a Nation achieved our universal enrolment as the half of the century has cross over? Have we as a nation achieved the Universal education besides advocating policies and central legislation at the centre?

The National Education day is goodwill gesture for our policy makers to re-thing of change in India's present system of education which is not at par with the desires of its children. At this moment, the nation is in need a vital agenda reach the hitherto uncovered populace with a new education policy with thrust on values and skills. The country's policy makers need to wake up and pledge on this National Education day for revolutionary changes in the system.

Life Sketch

Maulana Abul Kalam Muhiyuddin Ahmed was a Muslim scholar and a senior political leader of the Indian independence movement. He was one of the most prominent Muslim leaders to support Hindu-Muslim unity, opposing the partition of India on communal lines. Following India's independence, he became the first Minister of Education in the Indian government. He is commonly remembered as Maulana Azad; he had adopted Azad (Free) as his pen name.

As a young man, Azad composed poetry in Urdu as well as treatises on religion and philosophy. He rose to prominence through his work as a journalist, publishing works critical of the British Raj and espousing the causes of Indian nationalism. Azad became a leader of the *Kilafat Movement* during which he came into close contact with Indian leader Mahatma Gandhi. Azad became an enthusiastic supporter of Gandhi's ideas of non-violent civil disobedience, and worked actively to organize the Non-cooperation movement in protest of the 1919 Rowlatt Acts. Azad committed himself to Gandhi's ideals, including promoting Swadeshi (Indigenous) products and the cause of Swaraj (self-rule) for India. He would become the youngest person to serve as the President of the Indian National Congress in 1923.

Azad was one of the main organizers of the Dharasana Satyagraha in 1931, and emerged as one of the most important national leaders of the time, prominently leading the causes of Hindu-Muslim unity as well as espousing secularism and socialism. He served as Congress President from 1940 to 1945, during which the *Quit India* rebellion was launched and Azad was imprisoned with the entire Congress leadership for three years. Azad became the most prominent Muslim opponent of the demand for a separate Muslim state of Pakistan and served in the interim national government. Amidst communal turmoil following the partition of India, he worked for religious harmony. As India's Education Minister, Azad oversaw the establishment of a national education system with free primary education and modern institutions of higher education. He is also credited with the foundation of the University Grants Commission, an important institution to supervise and advance the higher education in the nation.

Azad's family descended from a line of eminent *Ulama* or scholars of Islam, hailing from *Herat, Afghanistan* and had settled in India during the reign of the Mughal emperor Babur. His mother was of Arab descent, the daughter of Shaikh Muhammad Zahir Watri and his father, Maulana Khairuddin was, then living in Bengal, was of Persian (Tajik) origin. The family lived in the Bengal region until Maulana Khairuddin left India during the Indian rebellion of 1857 and settled in Mecca, the holiest city in Islam, where he met his wife. The family returned to Kolkata in 1890 where his father earned a reputation as a learned Muslim scholar. Azad's mother died when he was 11 year old.

Azad was raised in an environment steeped in Islamic religion. He was given a traditional Islamic education, tutored at his home and in the neighbourhood mosque by his father and later religious scholars. Azad mastered several languages, including Urdu, Persian, Hindko, Arabic and Hindi. He was also trained in the subjects of mathematics, philosophy, world history and science by reputed tutors hired by his family. The Maulana interpreted scriptures from the rationalist point of view. Soaked in Islamic tradition and with many personal contacts with prominent Muslim leaders of Egypt, Turkey, Syria, Palestine, Iraq and Iran, he was profoundly affected by political and cultural developments in these countries.

He was known in Islamic countries probably more than any other Indian Muslim. At the age of 20 he went on a tour of Iraq, Syria and Egypt and met the young Turks and Arab nationalists including Christians. The tour proved very useful to Azad to crystallize his thoughts on the neo-colonialists who were exploiting those countries and how India could help them.

On return he stated a journal in Urdu named 'Al Hilal' in 1912. It was this journal where he aired his liberal views. 'Rationalist in outlook and profoundly versed in Islamic lore and history'.

Azad, with his Arabic mother tongue and orthodox family background, had to pursue a traditional Islamic education. But though 'he did not receive any modern education institutionally, through private studies and practice, he acquired proficiency in Urdu, Persian, Hindi and English. Like many other self-educational celebrities of his time, he taught himself world history and politics. He wrote many works, reinterpreting the Holy Quran, Hadith and *fiqh*. His erudition led him to repudiate *Taqliq* or the tradition of conformity and accept the principle of *Tajdid* or innovation. His concept of *tajdid* persuaded him to believe that all religions and ethnic peoples of India could make a happy federation of faiths and cultures within one independent state. This could, however, be possible only when, he believed, it would be based on democracy and secularism. In this regard, Azad was perhaps one of the earliest political thinkers of India to define and enunciate the idea of a secularist democracy for independent India.

As has been indicated already, by upbringing and education Azad was destined to be a clergyman. He mentions in his autobiography that most of his ancestors were religious divines. However, Azad had a political bent of mind. At a very early age he showed interest in politics. He developed interest in the pan-Islamic doctrines of Jamaluddin Afghani and the Aligarh thought of Sir Syed Ahmed Khan. Imbued with the pan-Islamic Spirit, he visited Afghanistan, Iraq, Egypt, Syria and Turkey. But he returned to Calcutta with an altogether new perception of life and politics.

Educational Contributions

The journal 'Al-Hilal' became extremely popular and in two years its circulation to 30,000. The inevitable happened when in 1914 the British Government confiscated the press and banned the journal under the Defence of India Act. Azad was arrested and sent to Ranchi jail where he suffered untold hardships. Released from jail he resumed his educational writings. He spoke in a new language, writs Nehru.

It was not only a new language in thought and approach, even its texture was different, for Azad's style was tense and virile though sometimes a little difficult because of its Persian background. He used new phrases for new ideas and was definite influence in giving shape to Urdu language as it is today. The older conservative Muslims did not react favourably to all this and criticized Azad's opinion and approach.

Yet not even the most learned of them could meet Azad in debate and argument, even on the basis of scriptures and tradition, for Azad's knowledge of these happened to be greater than theirs. He was a strange mixture of medieval scholasticism, eighteenth century rationalism and modern outlook. There were a few among the older generation who approved of Azad's writings, among them being Shibil and Sir Sayyaid of Aligarh University.

Among the new institutions he established were the three National Academies viz. the Sangeet Natak Academy (1953), Sahitya Academy (1954) and Lalit Kala Academy (1954), the Indian Council for Cultural Relations having been established by him earlier in 1950.

The Maulana felt that the cultural content in Indian Education was very low during the British rule and needs to be strengthened through curriculum. As Chairman of the Central Advisory Board of Education, an apex body to recommend to the Government educational reform both at the center and the states including universities, he advocated, in particular, universal primary education, free and compulsory for all children upto the age of 14, girls education, vocational training, agricultural education and technical education.

He established the University Grants Commission (UGC) in 1956 by an Act of Parliament for disbursement of grants and maintenance of standard Indian universities.

His greatest contribution, however, is that in spite of being an eminent scholar of Urdu, Persian and Arabic he stood for the retention of English language for educational advantages and national and international needs. However, primary education should be imparted in the mother-tongue.

On the technical education side, he strengthened the All India Council for Technical Education (AICTE). The Indian Institute of Technology, Kharagpur (IIT-K) was established in 1951 followed by a chain of IIT's at Bombay, Madras and Kanpur and Delhi. The School of Planning and Architecture (SPA) came into existence at Delhi in 1955.

Maulana Azad was a Muslim theologian of international repute, and one of the earliest to join the nationalist movement and to lead it steadfastly, arousing the ire of his communal-minded co-religionists. He was perhaps the only one among our leaders who was jailed during both World War I (1914-18) and II (1939-45) for campaigning for Swaraj.

During the most fateful days of the national struggle, he was the President of the Indian National Congress. Personally unwilling to accept the principle of the two-nation theory, he too, like Gandhiji, reluctantly reconciled himself to India's partition in 1947. He took active part in the agitation, joined the secret societies and revolutionary organization and came in contact with Sri Aurobindo Ghosh and Shyam Sundar Chakravarty.

Maulana Azad was a prolific writer with books in Urdu, Persian and Arabic notably amongst which is 'India Wins Freedom', his political biography, translated from Urdu to English. Maulana's translation of Quran from Arabic into Urdu in six volumes published by Sahitya Academy in 1977 is indeed his 'Magnum Opus'.

Since then several editions of 'Tarjaman-e-Quran' have come out. His other books include 'Gubar-e-Khatir'. 'Hijr-o-Vasal', 'Khatbat-Azadi', 'Hamari Azad', 'Tazkara'. He gave a new life to Anjamane-Tarrqui-e-Urdu-e-Hind'. Azad's tomb is located next to the Jama Masjid in Delhi. In recent years great concern has been expressed by many in India over the poor maintenance of the tomb. On November 16, 2005 the Delhi High Court ordered that the tomb of Maulana Azad in New Delhi be renovated and restored as a major national monument Azad's tomb is a major landmark and receives large number of visitors annually.

Azad- "Mir-i- Karawan" (the caravan leader)

A normal human tendency is to forget the past and march ahead. If one looks down upon those who had helped them when they confronted challenges an educational reformer proved to be different.

He had to face challenges in advocating a National System of Education. Infact, a recent circular of the Government of India to commemorate the birthday of Maulana Abul Kalam Azad on November 11, as National Education Day has raised many eyebrows in the country to re-organize the grim educational situation.

But if we look back to the historical developments of education in India, a man of enormous tastes, rated high in the realm of education, Maulana Abul Kalam Azad has all along played a prominent role in keeping the movement of education alive in this country.

Packed with several achievements, Maulana Azad oversaw the establishment of a national education system with free primary education and modern institutions of higher learning.

The very recent decision of the Union Ministry of HRD, Government of India to declare his birthday as National Education Day is a treatise on the live, struggle and contribution of the great educationist of the country. It would hopefully be of immense interest and inspiration for all the citizens, scholars, students, teachers and academicians, to imbibe his spirit of educational ideas among the current posterity of the nation.

The country's educationist has to learn from his outstanding contributions and policies. Maulana Abul Kalam Azad was the first to raises the issue of the National System of Education which is today the bed-roc of the National Policy on Education (1986) updated in 1992. The concept implies that up to a given level, all students, irrespective of caste, creed, location or sex have access to education of a comparable quality.

All educational programmes, he stressed, must be carried out in strict conformity with secular values and constitutional framework. He stood for a common educational structure of 10+2+3 throughout India.

If Maulana Azad were alive today he would have been happiest to see the Right to Free Education Bill and national flagship mission mode projects getting a Cabinet approval for the approval of Parliament. The Right to Education Bill seeks to make free and compulsory education a fundamental right.

The wealth of the nation, according to Maulana Azad, was not in the country's banks but in primary schools. Maulana was also a great votary of the concept of Neighbourhood schools and the Common School System. Maulana Abul Kalam Azad is one of those rare personalities through whom the distinctions of the 20th century can be recognized and possibilities of the 21st century determined.

He stood for a learning society through liberal, modern and universal education combining the humanism of Indian arts, a society where the strong are just and the weak secure. Where the youth is disciplined and the women lead a life of dignity– a non-violent, non-exploiting social and economic order. He was free India's First Education Minister and guided the destinies of the Nation of eleven years.

REFERENCES

1. Dash, B.N.—*A New Approach to Teacher & Education in the Emerging Indian Society*. Hyderabad: Neelkamal Publications Pvt. Ltd.
2. Russel, B. *Wisdom of West*. London Allen and Unwin.
3. Schofield, H. (1972). *The Philosophy of Education*. London: George Allen.
4. Sharma, Y.K.—*The Doctrines of the Great Indian Educators*. New Delhi: Kanishka Publishers, Distributors.
5. Sharma, Y.K.—*The Doctrines of the Great Western Educators From Plato to Bertrand Russell*. New Delhi: Kanishka Publishers, Distributors.
6. Sivarajan, K.—Education in the Emerging Indian Society. Calicut University, Central Co-Operative Stores.
7. Sodhi, T.S. *Philosophical Dimensions of Education*. Ambala: The Indian Publications.
8. Warnock, M. (1977). *Schools of Thought*. London: Faber and Faber.
9. Wynee. J.P. (1947). *Philosophies of Education*. London: Prentice Hall Inc.
10. www.wikipedia.com

14

Great Western Educators

PLATO

Plato (428/427 BC-348/347 BC), was a Classical Greek philosopher, mathematician, writer of philosophical dialogues and founder of the Academy in Athens, the first institution of higher learning in the Western world. Along with his mentor, Socrates and his student, Aristotle, Plato helped to lay the foundations of Western philosophy. Plato was originally a student of Socrates and was as much influenced by his thinking as by what he saw as his teacher's unjust death.

Plato's sophistication as a writer is evident in his Socratic dialogues; thirty-five dialogues and thirteen letters have traditionally been ascribed to him, although modern scholarship doubts the authenticity of at least some of these. Plato's writings have been published in several fashions; this has led to several conventions regarding the naming and referencing of Plato's texts.

Although there is little question that Plato lectured at the Academy that he founded, the pedagogical function of his dialogues, if any, is not known with certainty. The dialogues since Plato's time have been used to teach a range of subjects, mostly including philosophy, logic, rhetoric, mathematics and other subjects about which he wrote.

Life Sketch

Based on ancient sources, most modern scholars estimate that he was born in Athens or Aegina between 429 and 423 BC his father was Ariston. According to a disputed tradition, reported by Diogenes

Laertius, Ariston traced his descent from the king of Athens, Codrus and the king of Messenia, Melanthus. Plato's mother was Perictione, whose family boasted of a relationship with the famous Athenian lawmaker and lyric poet Solon. Perictione was sister of Charmides and niece of Critias, both prominent figures of the Thirty Tyrants, the brief oligarchic regime, which followed on the collapse of Athens at the end of the Peloponnesian War (404-403 BC). Besides Plato himself, Ariston and Perictione had three other children; these were two sons, Adeimantus and Glaucon and a daughter Potone, the mother of Speusippus (the nephew and successor of Plato as head of his philosophical Academy). According to the *Republic,* Adeimantus and Glaucon were older than Plato. Nevertheless, in his Memorabilia, Xenophon presents Glaucon as younger than Plato.

Ariston tried to force his attentions on Perictione, but failed of his purpose; then the ancient Greek god Apollo appeared to him in a vision and as a result of it, Ariston left Perictione unmolested. Another legend related that, while he was sleeping as an infant, bees had settled on the lips of Plato; an augury of the sweetness of style in which he would discourse philosophy.

Ariston appears to have died in Plato's childhood, although the precise dating of his death is difficult. Perictione then married Pyrilampes, her mother's brother, who had served many times as an ambassador to the Persian court and was a friend of Pericles, the leader of the democratic faction in Athens. Pyrilampes had a son from a previous marriage, Demus, who was famous for his beauty. Perictione gave birth to Pyrilampes' second son, Antiphon, the half-brother of Plato, who appears in *Parmenides.*

In contrast to his reticence about himself, Plato used to introduce his distinguished relatives into his dialogues, or to mention them with some precision: Charmides has one named after him; Critias speaks in both *Charmides* and *Protagoras;* Adeimantus and Glaucon take prominent parts in the *Republic.* From these and other references one can reconstruct his family tree and this suggests a considerable amount of family pride. According to Burnet, "the opening scene of the *Charmides* is a glorification of the whole [family] connection ... Plato's dialogues are not only a memorial to Socrates, but also the happier days of his own family."

Name: According to Diogenes Laërtius, the philosopher was named *Aristocles* after his grandfather, but his wrestling coach,

Ariston of Argos, dubbed him "Platon", meaning "broad," on account of his robust figure. According to the sources mentioned by Diogenes (all dating from the Alexandrian period), Plato derived his name from the breadth (*platytês*) of his eloquence, or else because he was very wide (*platýs*) across the forehead. In the 21st century some scholars disputed Diogenes and argued that the legend about his name being *Aristocles* originated in the Hellenistic age.

Education: Apuleius informs us that Speusippus praised Plato's quickness of mind and modesty as a boy and the "first fruits of his youth infused with hard work and love of study." Plato must have been instructed in grammar, music and gymnastics by the most distinguished teachers of his time. Dicaearchus went so far as to say that Plato wrestled at the Isthmian games. Plato had also attended courses of philosophy; before meeting Socrates, he first became acquainted with Cratylus (a disciple of Heraclitus, a prominent pre-Socratic Greek philosopher) and the Heraclitean.

Plato may have travelled in Italy, Sicily, Egypt and Cyrene. Said to have returned to Athens at the age of forty, Plato founded one of the earliest known organized schools in Western Civilization on a plot of land in the Grove of Hecademus or Academus. The Academy was "a large enclosure of ground which was once the property of a citizen at Athens named Academus... some, however, say that it received its name from an ancient hero" and it operated until AD 529, when it was closed by Justinian I of Byzantium, who saw it as a threat to the propagation of Christianity. Many intellectuals were schooled in the Academy, the most prominent one being Aristotle.

Main Publications

The Republic,The Laws, Protogoras and Symposium are his famous works.

Philosophy

Plato and Aristotle, a detail of *The School of Athens*, a fresco by Raphael. Aristotle gestures to the earth, representing his belief in knowledge through empirical observation and experience, while holding a copy of his *Nicomachean Ethics* in his hand. Plato holds his *Timaeus* and gestures to the heavens, representing his belief in The Forms.

Plato often discusses the father-son relationship and the "question" of whether a father's interest in his sons has much to do with how well his sons turn out. A boy in ancient Athens was socially located by his family identity and Plato often refers to his characters in terms of their paternal and fraternal relationships. Socrates was not a family man and saw himself as the son of his mother, who was apparently a midwife. A divine fatalist, Socrates mocks men who spent exorbitant fees on tutors and trainers for their sons and repeatedly ventures the idea that good character is a gift from the gods. Crito reminds Socrates that orphans are at the mercy of chance, but Socrates is unconcerned. In the *Theaetetus*, he is found recruiting as a disciple a young man whose inheritance has been squandered. Socrates twice compares the relationship of the older man and his boy lover to the father-son relationship (*Lysis* 213a, *Republic* 3.403b), and in the *Phaedo*, Socrates' disciples, towards whom he displays more concern than his biological sons, say they will feel "fatherless" when he is gone. Many dialogues, like these, suggest that man-boy love (which is "spiritual") is a wise man's substitute for father-son biology (which is "bodily").

In several dialogues, Socrates floats the idea that knowledge is a matter of recollection and not of learning, observation or study. He maintains this view somewhat at his own expense, because in many dialogues, Socrates complains of his forgetfulness. Socrates is often found arguing that knowledge is not empirical and that it comes from divine insight. He is quite consistent in believing in the immortality of the soul and several dialogues end with long speeches imagining the afterlife. More than one dialogue contrasts knowledge and opinion, perception and reality, nature and custom and body and soul. The only contrast to this is his Parmenides.

Several dialogues tackle questions about art: Socrates says that poetry is inspired by the muses and is not rational. He speaks approvingly of this and other forms of divine madness (drunkenness, eroticism and dreaming) in the *Phaedrus* (265a–c), and yet in the *Republic* wants to outlaw Homer's great poetry and laughter as well. In *Ion*, Socrates gives no hint of the disapproval of Homer that he expresses in the *Republic*. The dialogue *Ion* suggests that Homer's *Iliad* functioned in the ancient Greek world as the bible does today in the modern Christian world: as divinely inspired literature that can provide moral guidance, if only it can be properly interpreted.

On politics and art, religion and science, justice and medicine, virtue and vice, crime and punishment, pleasure and pain, rhetoric and rhapsody, human nature and sexuality, love and wisdom, Socrates and his company of disputants had something to say.

Educational Philosophy

Education should aim at achievement of the absolutes-beauty, goodness and truth. It should give to the body and soul all the perfection to which they are susceptible. In the Republic he describes an Ideal State that maintains social justice. The citizens of this state belong to three classes, viz. administrators, soldiers and farmers. The first two should be given education, the third one need no education at all.

The aims of education are inculcation of virtue and citizenship, development of the body and soul, vision of truth and appreciation of beauty. Music and Physical Education along with Mathematics and Geometry should be included in primary school curriculum. In higher education one should get Physical Education in addition to virtue and aesthetic sense developed through the study of Higher Mathematics, Geometry, Astronomy, Philosophy and Music.

ARISTOTLE–'THE MASTER OF THOSE WHO KNOW'

Life Sketch

Aristotle was born in 384 BC in the small township of 'Stagira' in the Northern Greece as the son of Nicomachus and Phalstis. Nicomachus was a doctor, friend and physician to king Amynitas of Maudon. In 367 BC at the age of 17 years, Aristotle moved to Athens and entered the famous 'academy' of Plato and stayed there as a student and teacher for 20 years. In 347 BC after the death of Plato, Aristotle left the academy and started travelling. He went to Assos in Hysia and from there to mitylene. He was called by King Philip to look after the education of his son Alexander (in 342 BC) who later become famous as Alexander the great. For seven years he was the tutor of Alexander, after which he returned to Athens to establish his school, 'Lycczum' it was also known as peripatetic school because of the habit of Aristotle of walking while lecturing. After the death of Alexander (323 BC), in 322 BC, Aristotle left Athens for Chala's or the Island of Eubora, where he died within a few months. The major influences on Aristotle were Plato and his years at the 'Academy'.

Works of Aristotle

Aristotle's works have been classified into those of logic, metaphysics, ethics, politics, psychology and natural sciences.

1. Logic:- 'Organism' (divided into different books).
2. Metaphy:- 'Metaphysics' (includes 14 books).
3. Ethics:- Nicomachean Ethics, (10 books), 'Endemian Ethics'.
4. Politics:- 'Politics' (8 books) on the constitution of Athens.
5. Psychology:- 'On the Soul' (8 books).
6. Natural Science:- 'Physics' (8 books)
   'Astronomy' (4 books)
   'Origin and Decay' (2 books)
   'Meteorology'
   'Cosmology'
   'Botany'
   'History of Animals' (10 books)
   'On the progression of Animals'
   'On the origin of Animals' (5 books)
   'On the 10 comotion of Animals'

From the point of view of the period of writing, Aristotle's works are classified into the following three periods.

1. Writings of Platonic Age—These were written during Aristotle's stay in Plato's Academy. Most important is 'on the soul'.
2. Writings in the court of Maudon—Most important are 'Metaphysics and Politics'.
3. Writings in Lycezum—Most important are 'on creation and Destruction', on Heaven's etc.

Philosophy of Aristotle

Aristotle rejected most of his master's (Plato) view on philosophy, especially those with regard to Ideas, Aristotle was of the view that 'material things' were also real as ideas because they conform the ideas. Aristotle spent more times in thinking about new things 'are' rather than how they ought to be. Aristotle can be said to be a materialist.

Aristotle not only enriched our motions about the world of matter, he did much to help us in our thinking-through his logic (E.g: theory of induction and deduction).

Aristotle thought that states come into existence, when families which exists to supply basic needs, combine to constitute a state, which exist for the sake of the good life. "The state is a creature of the nature", just as man is by nature a political animal."

Art for Aristotle is real, as real as what is represents. Art discloses the universal that lies hidden in every individual, it brings out the ideal in every material thing. According to him, tragedies, are about people 'better than ourselves", but comedies are about people "worse than ourselves." He preferred "Tragedies to comedies in this regard."

Philosophy of Education

This Goal or Purpose of Education

For Aristotle, the goal of Education is identical with the goal of man. Obviously all forms of education are explicitly or implicitly directed towards a human ideal. Aristotle considers that education is essential for the complete self-realization of man. For Aristotle, the happy man is neither a noble savage nor man in his natural state, but the educated man. The good man is a virtuous man, but virtue is acquired precisely through education. "The man who is to be good must be well trained and habituated."

"All Forms of Education Should Aim at the Mean", He observed. Freedom is one of the ultimate goals of education, for happiness is impossible without freedom. Such freedom is achieved through contemplation or the philosophical life, which is possible only through education.

Leisure or Schote (the etymological root of the word school) which should be the goal of education is the freedom to apply oneself to essential matters. It is the form of freedom that leads to wisdom a life devoted to philosophy and contemplation, that is true happiness. Through leisure, education should lead to man's ultimate goal, an intellectual life rooted in the mind. Man can attain this only through education.

Education has a conservative role for each society and each form of Government there exists a particular system of education. There is a system of education that corresponds to democracy, another that is 'appropriate for oligarchy. It is for this reason that education is the primary task of the legislation. Education at the state level must be an education for peace. Just as leisure is the goal of occupation, peace is the goal of war.

Education System

Aristotle devotes a great deal of space to the development of an education system in the description of the ideal city of Polis. Aristotle devices a veritable system of continuing education. Education is not limited to youth. It is a comprehensive process concerning the whole human person and lasting life time. This process is organized in periods of seven years. The first period (0-7 years) is that of preschool education. This is the responsibility of the parents, especially the father who is responsible for the existence of his children exercises are important at this stage. They should be trained through games. Between the ages of 5 and 7 they must be spectators of the lessons, they will learns afterwards.

At the age of 7, children enter to school. Divided into 3 cycles, formal schooling contains, upto the age of 21. However education is not completed at the age of 21.

Education, for Aristotle was the affair of the state. Schools should be public. The introduction of public education always indicates a certain democratization of education. According to him, 'Education must become and the Same for all'.

He prescribed some sort of vocational training for tradesmen. He even prescribed a form of education for slaves.

In his view, women are certainly not the equals of men. But he also envisaged public education for girls. Such education would be directed towards beauty and greatness, chastity and liking for work without greed.

Curriculum

Aristotle recognizes at least 4 subject's for instruction, i.e., grammar, physical training, music and drawing. His grammar might have included fundamentals of logic and mathematics. "Young people should be instructed in such useful acquirements" as are really necessary. Useful acquirements include grammar, physical training and drawing. For Aristotle, physical training is most important for the body; it must help to form character, courage and sense of honour.

"Education is the creation of sound mind in a sound body", he observed Music is a means of influencing moral character. Arts help to judge these beauty.

Methodology and Pedagogy

"Clearly, then there are 3 standards to which education should conform. They are the mean, the possible and the proper."

So, extremes and excesses are, above all, to be avoided. Education should be limited to what is appropriate for the pupil, taking into account this age, character and so on.

In accordance with man's nature, which is composed of the body, the soul and the reason, education should begin with physical training, continue with music and conclude with philosophy.

Aristotle identifies two complementary educational categories, i.e., education through reason and education through habit.

Education through habit for the things we have to learn before we can do them. E.g. Playing, moral education and science also (it is through the practice of science that the possession of science becomes learned in actuality). Education through habit is connected with 3 motions – imitation, experience and memory. Man likes to imitate, all the arts are based on an imitation of nature. Education through reason compliments education through habit. e.g.: Teaching of sciences, its aim is to impart an understanding of causes. To teach is to indicate the cause of all things. Education through reason is concerned with the universal which surpasses experience – "Men of experience know- that a thing is, but they do not know, why it is, where as men of learning know the reason and the cause."

Education through reason is characterized by two methods: epagoge or learning by induction and learning by demonstration.... Demonstration proceeds on the basis of particular cases. Aristotle's 'epagogue pedagogy' is a form of teaching that proceeds from example to an understanding of causes, as in science. The theoretical sciences-Mathematics, Physics and theology are chiefly taught by demonstration. Thus to a great extent, education through reason coincides with the scientific approach or theoretical philosophy, just as education through habit coincides with ethical action or practical philosophy.

Contributions

1. Pupil as great as 'Alexander'
2. Lycezum-school
3. Writings

4. Logical thought (Induction, Deduction)
5. Thoughts on metaphysics
6. Philosophy of science
7. Ethics
8. Politics
9. Rhetoric
10. Poetics and thoughts on literature
11. Thoughts on education.

IMMANUEL KANT (1724-1804)

Immanuel Kant was one of the important philosophers who lived during the 18th century in Germany. Experts in the history of German education describe the 18th century as the age of Pedagogies. Kant like many others, turned his attention to education, but his significance in his particular sector can only be appreciated against the more general background of his philosophy.

Life Sketch

Kant (1724-1804) the founder of German realism is generally considered the greatest of modern philosophers. He was born in Konigsberg on 22nd April 1724. His parents belonged to the lower middle class. He acquired the basic skills of reading and writing at the Hospital school in Konigsberg. In 1740, at the age of 16, Kant was admitted to the University of Konigsberg, qualifying in the same years as a university teacher with his dissertation. On 'New light' on the first principles of Metaphysical cognition. Kant died in 1804.

What is Education

Kant subscribed to the fundamental pedagogical position that education is imperative for the development of man kind. Man is that which education makes of him and nothing more. It will be noted that man is always educated by other men who have themselves been educated previously. Education may be firstly in empirical terms—in the manner in which education process takes place in a given real situation. Secondly it must be considered in its anthropological and with reference to its normative idea. The provision of true and good education holds the great secret of the true perfection of human nature. Good education is itself the source of all that is good in the world. Therefore we arrive at the conceptual principle that children must not be educated simply to achieve the present level but towards a possible better future level of the human race, in other words, taking account of the idea of man kind and the universal destiny of man. Good education is capable of bringing about a gradual improvement in the world. Kant names the following as the main tasks of education.

(a) Disciplined thinking
(b) Creation of a cultural outlook
(c) Enhancement of civilization
(d) Imparting moral rectitude

Kant's fundamental way of thinking can be perceived in the definition of the fourth main function of education. Children must be educated to perform *(a)* Their duties to themselves and *(b)* Their duties to others, the duty to oneself, however, reside in the fact that the human being preservers the dignity of mankind in his own person. In all his actions, the child or the person to be educated must have in mind the fact that the human being bears within him a certain dignity, which makes him more noble them all others farms of life. His principle of obedience in education is always applied in the context of enlightened reason.

For Whom is Education Intended

Two levels of statements must be considered here, firstly, statements on human beings in general which are applicable to all age groups and secondly statements relating to children and adolescents who are not yet adults.

The true nature of a man is reflected in certain forces of the mind and understanding. Judgement is the application of the universal to the particular. Reason means the ability to perceive the relationship between the universal and the particular.

Nature of Discipline

The nature of the problem of discipline in this context is that the child must always remain aware of its freedom when disciplinary measures are taken, without obstructing the freedom of others. Children should be accustomed to work without and having to abandon play. In brief education must be made obligatory without becoming a form of slavery.

On these bases Kant reminds us of the following basic concepts:

The individual learns most thoroughly and best retain those things which he learns as it mere for himself. Learning to think can best be achieved using the Socratic method and not by what may be termed as mechanical. Importance was given to duty and action. Kant's theory of duty was deeply rooted in his notion of world citizenship.

Methods

The research instruments available to contemporary science are many and varied as a result of a long process of historical development. Kant passed the way for one fundamental position of modern enlightened educational science which starts out from the principle of the freedom of its subject. Even it there had been no notion of freedom before him, that freedom has existed as a normative idea some Kant's day unaffected by all negative empirical factors and realities of repression.

Impact of Kant's Works

As an education, Kant's contribution can be classified as basic education, family education, school education, university education, general education, adult education, education of senior citizens. Kant gave rise to German idealism. He was a leading critical figure in the Prussian branch of human enlightenment in the 1st century. It is still possible to highlight the impact of Kant's educational theories from 2 angles, 1st from the angle of the connotations and 2nd from its negative attributes. Since the days of Kant, the term 'person' has reflected, the fact that all human beings are an end in themselves, i.e., that regardless of class, world view, religion, race, nation etc. and of all obstacles standing in the way, each person is from the start of his existence a reality in his own right and with his own dignity. Kant's quadruple presents of it was the main task of education. He supported for the in human principles of obedience which has been constant feature of Prussian history on the contrary, he sought to give expression to the fact that all educational activities must be of shaped with reference the principle of ones own understanding in the various phases of education.

JEAN-JACQUES ROUSSEAU

Life Sketch

Jean Jacques Rousseau (Geneva, 28 June 1712—Ermenonville, 2 July 1778) was a major philosopher, writer and composer of the eighteenth century Enlightenment, whose political philosophy influenced the French Revolution and the development of modern political and educational thought. His novel, *Emile: or, On Education,* which he considered his most important work, is a seminal treatise on the education of the whole person for citizenship.

Rousseau's father, Isaac Rousseau, was a watchmaker who, notwithstanding his artisan status, was well educated and a lover of music. Rousseau's mother, Suzanne Bernard Rousseau, the daughter of a Calvinist preacher, died of birth complications nine days after his birth. He and his older brother François were brought up by their father and a paternal aunt, also named Suzanne.

When Jean Jacques Rousseau was ten, his father, an avid hunter, got into a legal quarrel with a wealthy landowner on whose lands he had been caught trespassing. To avoid certain defeat in the courts, he moved away to Nyon in the territory of Bern, taking Rousseau's aunt Suzanne with him. He remarried and from that point Jean-Jacques saw little of him. Jean-Jacques was left in with his maternal uncle, who packed him, along with his own son, Abraham Bernard, away to board for two years with a Calvinist Minister in a hamlet outside of Geneva.

At school he was punnished quite often and this hurt him very much. For a few months Rousseau worked in the office of the registrar of the city. He soon left the job and began to roam about till he was thirty, when he came back to Paris and got married. But he left his family of five children and started leading a new life for the pursuit of truth. His teachings were found revolutionary and he was watched by the French authorities. So he left for Switzerland and later died while he was in England.

Philosophy

Rousseau was the champion of naturalism and pleaded for liberty, fraternity and equality. In Emile, we can see a detailed description of his educational ideas. According to Rousseau education is a process of developing in to an enjoyable, rational, harmoniously blended, useful and hence natural life. To live is not merely to breathe; it is to act, to make use of our organs, sences, our faculties and of all those are ours, which in turn will give us the feeling of an existence. Discipline is acquired only by natural consequences.

Educational Philosophy

According to Rousseau education is life itself, not a preparation for a future stage in life. Education should result in real development i.e., development of the nature and virtues of the learner to the highest level.

Main Publications

Rousseau published a number of essays and books. *The Progress of Arts and Sciences, The New Heloise, The Social Contract, Emile* are some of them.

JOHANN HEINRICH PESTALOZZI

Life Sketch

Coat of arms of Pestalozzi's family from Zürich. He was born on January 12, 1746 in Zürich, Switzerland. His father died when he was young and he was brought up by his mother. At the University of Zürich he associated himself with Lavater and the party of reform. His earliest years were spent in schemes for improving the condition of the people. The death of his friend Johann Kaspar Bluntschli turned him from politics, however and induced him to devote himself to education. He married Anna Schulthess in 1769 at twenty-three and bought a piece of waste land at Birr, Aargau called Neuhof (New Farm), where he attempted the cultivation of madder. Pestalozzi knew nothing of business and the plan failed. Before this he had opened his farm-house as a school, but that plan also met with failure.

His first published book was *The Evening Hours of a Hermit* (1780), a series of aphorisms and reflections. This was followed by his masterpiece, *Leonard and Gertrude* (1781), an account of the gradual reformation, first of a household and then of a whole village, by the efforts of a good and devoted woman. It was avidly read in Germany and the name of Pestalozzi was rescued from obscurity.

During the French invasion of Switzerland in 1798, a number of orphaned children had been left without food or shelter in the Canton of Nidwalden. Pestalozzi took some of them under his charge and he converted a deserted convent into a school for them. During the winter he personally tended them with the utmost devotion, but in June 1799 the building was requisitioned by the French to use as a hospital and his charges were dispersed.

Philosophy

Pestalozzi was not a theoretical philosopher. His life itself was his work beyond all theory Pestalozzi is acclaimed as a practical educator. He enunciated psychological principles of teaching rather than philosophical ideas. As much, one can't find much by way of Pestalozzian philosophy. He was a man who stuggled hard and believed in alleviation of misery among the poor and the down-trodden, through a healthy system of education. He emphasised the value of individual and social experiences gained by learners under the guidance of competent educators.

Educational Philosophy

The educational philosophy of Pestalozzi can be summarised as follows:

- A good home is the ideal educational institution, for it is the centre of love of active co-operation.
- Schools are necessary since homes can't provide everything.
- The harmonious development of all the powers of the individual is the aim of education.
- Education is to be social and universal.
- Instruction is to be psychological.
- Instruction is to be imparted by way of observation and graded activities.
- Curriculum must be expanded along practical and scientific lines.
- Teaching is a skilled occupation and a moral vocation.

Main Publications

Pestalozzi wrote a number of books. *How Gertrude her Children, Books for Mothers, Mother and Child* etc. are his important books.

FRIEDRICH WILHELM AUGUST FROEBEL

Life Sketch

Friedrich Wilhelm August Froebel (April 21, 1782 – June 21, 1852) was a German pedagogue, a student of Pestalozzi who laid the foundation for modern education based on the recognition that children have unique needs and capabilities. He created the concept of the "kindergarten", and also coined the word now used in German and English. Friedrich Froebel was born at Oberweißbach in the

Principality of Schwarzburg-Rudolstadt in Thuringia. His father, who died in 1802, was the pastor of the orthodox Lutheran (alt-lutherisch) parish there. The church and Lutheran Christian faith were pillars in Froebel's own early education. Oberweißbach was a wealthy village in the Thuringian Forest and had been known centuries long for its natural herb remedies, tinctures, bitters, soaps and salves. Families had their own inherited areas of the forest where herbs and roots were grown and harvested. Each family prepared, bottled and produced their individual products which were taken throughout Europe on trade routes passed from father to son, who were affectionately called "Buckelapotheker" or *Rucksack Pharmacists.* They adorned the church with art acquired from their travels, many pieces of which can still be seen in the renovated structure. The pulpit from which Froebel heard his father preach is the largest in all Europe and can fit a pastor and 12 men, a direct reference to Christ's apostles.

Shortly after Froebel's birth, his mother's health began to fail. She died when he was nine months old, profoundly influencing his life. In 1792, Froebel went to live in the small town of Stadt-Ilm with his uncle, a gentle and affectionate man. At the age of 15 Froebel, who loved nature, became the apprentice to a forester. In 1799, he decided to leave his apprenticeship and study mathematics and botany in Jena. From 1802 to 1805, he worked as a land surveyor.

On 11 September 1818, Froebel wed Wilhelmine Henriette Hoffmeister (b. 1780) in Berlin. The union was childless. Wilhelmine died in 1839, and Froebel married again in 1851. His second wife was Louise Levin.

Philosophy

He began as an educator in 1805 at the *Musterschule* (a secondary school) in Frankfurt, where he learnt about Johann Heinrich Pestalozzi's ideas. He later worked with Pestalozzi in Switzerland where his ideas further developed. From 1806 Froebel was the live-in teacher for a Frankfurt noble family's three sons. He lived with the three children from 1808 to 1810 at Pestalozzi's institute in Yverdon-les-Bains in Switzerland.

In 1811, Froebel once again went back to school in Göttingen and Berlin, eventually leaving without earning a certificate. He became a teacher at the *Plamannsche Schule* in Berlin, a boarding school for boys and at that time also a pedagogical and patriotic centre.

During his service in the Lützow Free Corps in 1813 and 1814– when he was involved in two campaigns against Napoleon – Fröbel befriended Wilhelm Middendorf, a theologian and fellow pedagogue and Heinrich Langethal, also a pedagogue.

Allgemeine Deutsche Erziehungsanstalt in Keilhau, nowadays the Keilhau Free Froebel School.

After Waterloo and the Congress of Vienna, Froebel found himself a civilian once again and became an assistant at the Museum of Mineralogy under Prof. Weiß. This did not, however, last very long and by 1816 he had quit and founded the *Allgemeine Deutsche Erziehungsanstalt* ("German General Education Institute") in Griesheim near Arnstadt in Thuringia. A year later he moved this to Keilhau near Rudolstadt. In 1831, work was continued there by the other cofounders Wilhelm Middendorf and Heinrich Langethal.

In 1820, Froebel published the first of his five Keilhau pamphlets, *An unser deutsches Volk* ("To Our German People"). The other four were published between then and 1823.

In 1826 he published is main literary work, *Die Menschenerziehung* ("The Education of Man") and founded the weekly publication *Die erziehenden Familien* ("The Educating Families"). In 1828 and 1829 he pursued plans for a people's education institute (*Volkserziehungsanstalt*) in Helba (nowadays a constituent community of Meiningen), but they were never realized.

From 1831 to 1836, Fröbel once again lived in Switzerland. In 1831 he founded an educational institute in Wartensee (Lucerne). In 1833 he moved this to Willisau and from 1835 to 1836, he headed the orphanage in Burgdorf (Berne), where he also published the magazine *Grundzüge der Menschenerziehung* ("Features of Human Education"). In 1836 appeared his work *Erneuerung des Lebens erfordert das neue Jahr 1836* ("The New Year 1836 Calls For the Renewal of Life").

He returned to Germany, dedicated himself almost exclusively to preschool child education and began manufacturing playing materials in Bad Blankenburg. In 1837 he founded a "care, playing and activity institute for small children in Bad Blankenburg. From

1838 to 1840 he also published the magazine *Ein Sonntagsblatt für Gleichgesinnte* ("A Sunday Paper for the Like-Minded").

In 1840 he coined the word kindergarten for the Play and Activity Institute he had founded in 1837 at Bad Blankenburg for young children, together with Wilhelm Middendorf and Heinrich Langethal. These two men were Fröbel's most faithful colleagues when his ideas were also transplanted to Keilhau near Rudolstadt.

He designed the educational play materials known as Froebel Gifts or *Fröbelgaben*, which included geometric building blocks and pattern activity blocks. A book entitled *Inventing Kindergarten*, by Norman Brosterman, examines the influence of Friedrich Froebel on Frank Lloyd Wright and modern art.

Friedrich Froebel's great insight was to recognise the importance of the activity of the child in learning. He introduced the concept of "free work" (*Freiarbeit*) into pedagogy and established the "game" as the typical form that life took in childhood and also the game's educational worth. Activities in the first kindergarten included singing, dancing, gardening and self-directed play with the Froebel Gifts. Froebel intended, with his *Mutter- und Koselieder* – a songbook that he published – to introduce the young child into the adult world.

These ideas about childhood development and education were introduced to academic and royal circles through the tireless efforts of his greatest proponent, the Baroness (Freiherrin) Bertha Marie von Marenholtz-Bülow. Through her Froebel made the acquaintance of the Royal House of the Netherlands, various Thuringian dukes and duchesses, including the Romanov wife of the Grand Duke von Sachsen-Weimar. Baroness von Marenholtz-Bülow, Duke von Meiningen and Froebel gathered donations to support art education for children in honour of the 100th anniversary of the birth of Goethe. The Duke of Meiningen granted the use of his hunting lodge, called Marienthal (the Vale of Mary) in the resort town of Bad Liebenstein for Froebel to train the first women as Kindergarten teachers (called *Kindergärtnerinnen*).

Froebel died on 21 June 1852 in Mariental. His grave is still found at the cemetery at Schweina, where his widow, who died in Hamburg, was also buried on 10 January 1900.

Educational Philosophy

Many ideas in the educational philosophy of Froebel were the outcomes of his philosophy of life as applied in education. The aim of education is to enable the child to realise the unity principles. Self activity is the method of education. The innate tendancies of the child have to be developed through self activity. The purpose of education is to unfold the innate powers of children in order to enable them to attain spiritual union with God. He believed in the innate goodness of the child. Education should lead to moral, religious and spiritual development.

Main Publications

He published many books on education. The education of Man, The Pedagogies of kindergarten, Mother's Play and Nursery Songs, Education and Development etc. are the main publications.

MARIA MONTESSORI

Life Sketch and Philosophy

Maria Montessori (August 31, 1870 – May 6, 1952) was an Italian physician, educator, philosopher, humanitarian and devout Catholic; she is best known for her philosophy and the Montessori method of education of children from birth to adolescence. Her educational method is in use today in a number of public as well as private schools throughout the world. Maria Montessori was born in Chiaravalle (Ancona), Italy to Alessandro Montessori and Renilde Stoppani (niece of Antonio Stoppani). At the age of thirteen she attended an all-boy technical school in preparation for her dreams of becoming an engineer. Montessori was the first woman to graduate from the University of Rome La Sapienza Medical School, becoming the first female doctor in Italy. She was a member of the University's Psychiatric Clinic and became intrigued with trying to educate the "mentally retarded" or "unhappy little ones" and the "uneducatable" in Rome. In 1896, she gave a lecture at the Educational Congress in Torino about the training of the disabled. The Italian Minister of Education was in attendance and was impressed by her arguments sufficiently to appoint her the same year as Director of the Scuola Ortofrenica, an institution devoted to the care and education of the mentally retarded. She accepted, in order to put her theories to proof. Her first notable success was to have several of her

8 year old students apply to take the State examinations for reading and writing. The "defective" children not only passed, but had above-average scores, an achievement described as "the first Montessori miracle." Montessori's response to their success was "if mentally disabled children could be brought to the level of normal children then (she) wanted to study the potential of 'normal' children."

"Scientific observation has established that education is not what the teacher gives; education is a natural process spontaneously carried out by the human individual and is acquired not by listening to words but by experiences upon the environment. The task of the teacher becomes that of preparing a series of motives of cultural activity, spread over a specially prepared environment and then refraining from obtrusive interference. Human teachers can only help the great work that is being done, as servants help the master. Doing so, they will be witnesses to the unfolding of the human soul and to the rising of a New Man who will not be a victim of events, but will have the clarity of vision to direct and shape the future of human society."

Because of her success with these children, she was asked to start a school for children in a housing project in Rome, which opened on January 6, 1907 and which she called "Casa dei Bambini" or Children's House. Children's House was a child care centre in an apartment building in the poor neighbourhood of Rome. She was focused on teaching the students ways to develop their own skills at a pace they set, which was a principle Montessori called "spontaneous self-development." A wide variety of special equipment of increasing complexity is used to help direct the interests of the child and hasten development. When a child is ready to learn new and more difficult tasks, the teacher guides the child's first endeavours in order to avoid wasted effort and the learning of wrong habits; otherwise the child learns alone. It has been reported that the Montessori method of teaching has enabled children to learn to read and write much more quickly and with greater facility than has otherwise been possible. The Montessori Method of teaching concentrates on quality rather than quantity. The success of this school sparked the opening of many more and a worldwide interest in Montessori's methods of education. After the 1907 establishment of Montessori's first school in Rome, by 1917 there was an intense interest in her method in North America, which later waned, in large part due to the publication of a small booklet entitled "The Montessori System Examined" by Kirkpatrick- a follower of John Dewey. (Nancy McCormick Rambusch contributed to the revival of the method in America by establishing the American Montessori Society in 1960); at the same time Margaret Stephenson came to the US from Europe and began a long history of training Montessori teachers under the auspices of the Association Montessori Internationale (AMI). Montessori was exiled by Mussolini mostly because she refused to compromise her principles and make the children into soldiers. She moved to Spain and lived there until 1936 when the Spanish Civil War broke out. She then moved to the Netherlands until 1939.

In the year 1939, the Theosophical Society of India extended an invitation asking Maria Montessori to visit India. She accepted the invitation and reached India the very same year accompanied by her only son, Mario Montessori Sr. This heralded the beginning of her special relationship with India. She made the international Headquarters of the Theosophical Society at Adyar, Chennai, her home. However the war forced her to extend her stay in India. With the help of her son, Mario, she conducted sixteen batches of courses called the Indian Montessori Training Courses. These courses laid a strong foundation for the Montessori Movement in India. In 1949 when she left for The Netherlands she appointed Albert Max Joosten as her personal representative and assigned him the responsibility of conducting the Indian Montessori Training Courses. Joosten along with Swamy S R, another disciple of Dr. Maria Montessori, continued the good work and ensured that the Montessori Movement in India was on a sound footing. During a teachers conference in India she was interned by the authorities and lived there for the duration of the war. Montessori lived out the remainder of her life in the Netherlands, which now hosts the headquarters of the AMI, or *Association Montessori Internationale*. She died in Noordwijk aan Zee. Her son Mario headed the AMI until his death in 1982.

Maria Montessori died in the Netherlands in 1952, after a lifetime devoted to the study of child development. Her early work centered on women's rights and social reform and evolved to encompass a totally innovative approach to education. Her success in Italy led to international recognition and for over 40 years she travelled all over the world, lecturing, writing and establishing training programmes.

In later years, 'Educate for Peace' became a guiding principle, which underpinned her work.

Educational Philosophy

The child is a body it grows and a soul which develops. If any educational activity is to be efficient, it should cater to the complete, unfolding of the childs individuality. The school must promote free and natural activities of the child if he is to benefit from education. Discipline must come through liberty.

Main Publications

Dr. Maria Montessori wrote a number of books on education. *The Discovery of the Child, Education for a New World, The Secret of Education, Child Training, The Child's Place and Education, Reconstruction in Education, The Montessori Method, The Advanced Montessori Method* etc. are some of her works.

JOHN DEWEY

Life Sketch and Philosophy

John Dewey (October 20, 1859—June 1, 1952) was an American philosopher, psychologist and educational reformer whose thoughts and ideas have been highly influential in the United States and around the world. Dewey, along with Charles Sanders Peirce and William James, is recognized as one of the founders of the philosophical school of pragmatism. He is also one of the founders of functional psychology and was a leading representative of the progressive movement in U.S. schooling during the first half of the 20th century.

Although Dewey is best known for his works on education, he also wrote on a wide range of subjects, including experience and nature, art and experience, logic and inquiry, democracy and ethics.

In his advocacy of democracy, Dewey considered two fundamental elements-schools and civil society-as being key areas needing attention and reconstruction to encourage experimental intelligence and plurality. In the necessary reconstruction of civil society, Dewey asserted that full democracy was to be obtained not just by extending voting rights but also by ensuring that there exists a fully-formed public opinion, accomplished by effective communication among citizens, experts and politicians, with the latter being held accountable for the policies they adopt.

Dewey was born in Burlington, Vermont of modest family origins. Like his older brother, Davis Rich Dewey, he attended the University of Vermont, from which he graduated (Phi Beta Kappa) in 1879. After three years as a high school teacher in Oil City, Pennsylvania, Dewey decided that he was unsuited for employment in primary or secondary education. After studying one year under G. Stanley Hall, working in the first American Laboratory of Psychology, Dewey received his Ph.D. from the School of Arts and Sciences at Johns Hopkins University in 1884, he took a faculty position at the University of Michigan (1884-88 and 1889-94) with the help of George Sylvester Morris. His unpublished and now lost dissertation was titled "The Psychology of Kant" and he made a special study of Hegel's Absolute idealism.

In 1894 Dewey joined the newly founded University of Chicago (1894-1904) where he shaped his belief in an empirically based theory of knowledge aligning his ideals with the newly emerging Pragmatic school of thought. His time at the University of Chicago resulted in four essays collectively entitled *Thought and its Subject-Matter* which was published with collected works from his colleagues at Chicago under the collective title *Studies in Logical Theory* (1903). During this time Dewey also founded the University of Chicago Laboratory Schools where he was able to actualize his pedagogical beliefs which provided material for his first major work on education, *The School and Society* (1899). Disagreements with the administration ultimately led to his resignation from the University at which point he left for the East Coast. In 1899, John Dewey was elected President of the American Psychological Association. From 1904 until his death he was Professor of philosophy at both Columbia University and Teachers College, Columbia University. In 1905 he became President of the American Philosophical Association. He was a long-time member of the American Federation of Teachers.

Educational Philosophy

Pragmatism in education is John Dewey's main contribution. He was influenced by the philosophy of Hegal in his early days and William James in his later days. His philosophy is a combination of Darwin's theory of evolution and William James's theory of pragmatism. So, experience has become the core of his philosophy. Practical side of life is more relevant here. He considers truth as a force which fulfiles the purposes of life.

Main Publications

John Dewey published a number of books on Education, Philosophy, Psychology, Ethics and Political Science. *The School and Society, The School and the Child, School of Tomorrow, Education Today, Democracy and Education, Moral Principles of Education* etc. are his famous works.

Educational Contributions

- Emphasis on the relation of the school, community and education with the realities of life.
- Stress on social aspects of education.
- Stress given to experiments and experiences in the curriculum.
- Emphasis on psychological and social aspect of education.
- Emphasis on the project method.
- Emphasis on critical thinking.

PAULO FREIRE

Life Sketch

Paulo Freire (Recife, Brazil September 19, 1921 – São Paulo, Brazil May 2, 1997) was a Brazilian educator and influential theorist of critical pedagogy Born on September 19, 1921 to middle class parents in Recife, Brazil, Freire became familiar with poverty and hunger during the 1929 Great Depression. These experiences, though brief, would shape his concerns for the poor and would help to construct his particular educational viewpoint.

Freire enrolled at Law School at the University of Recife in 1943. He also studied philosophy, more specifically phenomenology and the psychology of language. Although admitted to the legal bar, he never actually practiced law but instead worked as a teacher in secondary schools teaching Portuguese. In 1944, he married Elza Maia Costa de Oliveira, a fellow teacher. The two worked together for the rest of their lives and had five children.

In 1946, Freire was appointed Director of the Department of Education and Culture of the Social Service in the State of Pernambuco, the Brazilian state of which Recife is the capital.

In 1961, he was appointed Director of the Department of Cultural Extension of Recife University and in 1962 he had the first opportunity for significant application of his theories, when 300 sugarcane workers were taught to read and write in just 45 days. In response to this experiment, the Brazilian government approved the creation of thousands of cultural circles across the country.

In 1964, a military coup put an end to that effort. Freire was imprisoned as a traitor for 70 days. After a brief exile in Bolivia, Freire worked in Chile for five years for the Christian Democratic Agrarian Reform Movement and the Food and Agriculture Organization of the United Nations. In 1967, Freire published his first book, *Education as the Practice of Freedom*. He followed this with his most famous book, *Pedagogy of the Oppressed*, first published in Portuguese in 1968.

On the strength of reception of his work, Freire was offered a visiting professorship at Harvard University in 1969. The next year, *Pedagogy of the Oppressed* was published in both Spanish and English, vastly expanding its reach. Because of the political feud between Freire, a Christian socialist, and the successive authoritarian military dictatorships, it wasn't published in his own country of Brazil until 1974, when General Ernesto Geisel took control of Brazil and began his process of cultural liberalisation.

After a year in Cambridge, Massachusetts, USA Freire moved to Geneva, Switzerland to work as a special education advisor to the World Council of Churches. During this time Freire acted as an advisor on education reform in former Portuguese colonies in Africa, particularly Guinea Bissau and Mozambique.

In 1979, he was able to return to Brazil and moved back in 1980. Freire joined the Workers' Party (PT) in the city of Sao Paulo and acted as a supervisor for its adult literacy project from 1980 to 1986. When the PT prevailed in the municipal elections in 1988, Freire was appointed Secretary of Education for Sao Paulo.

In 1986, his wife Elza died. Freire married Maria Araújo Freire, who continues with her own educational work.

Freire died of heart failure on May 2, 1997.

Philosophy

Those who attempt to reddress the ill of the suffering of humanity are not leaders who work for the people, but who work with the people as their servents. This is Freire's philosophy which he preferes to be known as scientific revolutionary humanism. This is essentially a philosophy involving techniques of adult and nonformal education, through the message is applicable to any form of education.

Educational Contributions

"There is no such thing as a neutral education process. Education either functions as an instrument which is used to facilitate the integration of generations into the logic of the present system and bring about conformity to it, or it becomes the 'practice of freedom', the means by which men and women deal critically with reality and discover how to participate in the transformation of their world."

Paulo Freire contributed a philosophy of education that came not only from the more classical approaches stemming from Plato, but also from modern Marxist and anti-colonialist thinkers. In fact, in many ways his *Pedagogy of the Oppressed* may be best read as an extension of, or reply to, Frantz Fanon's *The Wretched of the Earth*, which emphasized the need to provide native populations with an education which was simultaneously new and modern (rather than traditional) and anti-colonial (not simply an extension of the culture of the colonizer).

Freire is best-known for his attack on what he called the "banking" concept of education, in which the student was viewed as an empty account to be filled by the teacher. The basic critique was not new—Rousseau's conception of the child as an active learner was already a step away from tabula rasa (which is basically the same as the "banking concept") and thinkers like John Dewey were strongly critical of the transmission of mere "facts" as the goal of education. Freire's work, however, updated the concept and placed it in context with current theories and practices of education, laying the foundation for what is now called critical pedagogy.

More challenging is Freire's strong aversion to the teacher-student dichotomy. This dichotomy is admitted in Rousseau and constrained in Dewey, but Freire comes close to insisting that it should be completely abolished. This is hard to imagine in absolute terms, since there must be some enactment of the teacher-student relationship in the parent-child relationship, but what Freire suggests is that a deep reciprocity be inserted into our notions of teacher and student. Freire wants us to think in terms of teacher-student and student-teacher - that is, a teacher who learns and a learner who teaches - as the basic roles of classroom participation.

This is one of the few attempts anywhere to implement something like democracy as an educational method and not merely a goal of democratic education. Even Dewey, for whom democracy was a touchstone, did not integrate democratic practices fully into his methods, though this was in part a function of Dewey's attitudes toward individuality. In its strongest early form this kind of classroom has been criticized on the grounds that it can mask rather than overcome the teacher's authority.

Freire's work has also been subject to criticism. Rich Gibson has critiqued his work as a cul-de-sac, a combination of old-style socialism (wherever Freire was not) and liberal reformism (wherever Freire was). Paul V. Taylor, in his "Texts of Paulo Freire," comes close to calling Freire a plagiarist, while Gibson notes Freire borrows heavily from Hegel's "Phenomenology." Gibson's dissertation which examines Freire's theory, practice and history in a Marxist context is the sharpest critique of Freire to date.

Main Publications

Paulo Freire summarised his philosophy, methods of work and the abstract realities of his working environment in a book titled 'Pedagogy of the Oppressed'. 'Cultural Action for Freedom' is another famous book.

HERBART SPENCER (1820-1903)

Life Sketch

Herbart Spencer was born in 25th April 1820 at Derby in England. In both lines his ancestors were nonconformists or Dissenters. His father was a learned man of science and engaged in the teaching profession. His uncle was also a teacher. Herbart was a lazy boy and at the age of 13, he was sent to Hinton to study under his uncle. He first ran away from there and returned and stayed for three years. He was not fortunate enough as to acquire higher education. In fact he could not concentrate on it and left it, but self-study was very dear to him and he continued with it for the whole of his life and this gave him a good deal of knowledge. Spencer never finished any book of even science, his favourite field. He picked them up for most part, by direct observation than by reading.

Spencer worked for his living and his profession intensified the practical tendency of his thought. He was surveyor, supervisor and designer of railway lines and bridges and in general, an engineer.

For a time he was a vegetarian, but he abandoned it when he saw a fellow-vegetarian, develop anemia and himself losing strength. He was ready to give everything a trial. His character had the defects of its virtues. "I am never puzzled", he tell us. His solitary bachelor life left him lacking in the warmly human qualities, though he could be inelegantly humane. He was so busy analyzing and describing life that he had no time to live it.

Spencer had an exceptionally logical mind. He was the clearest expositor of complex subjects that modern history can show, he wrote of difficult problems in terms so lucid that for a generation all the world was interested in philosophy. He loned spacious generalizations and made his works interesting rather with his hypotheses than with his proofs.

The first book written by him was social statistics; later he made many more contributions. His fame vanished and he was saddened during his last years: scientific specialists whose privileged fields he had invaded dornned him with faint praise, ignoring his contributions and emphasizing his errors. He was incorrigibly sincere and offended every group by speaking candidly on every subject. As he aged, he become more gentle in opposition and more moderate in opinion. Looking back ones his arduous career, he thought himself foolish for having sought literacy fame instead of the simples pleasure of life when he died in 1903, he had come to think that his work had been done in vain.

Spencer's Philosophy of Life

Various scientific inventions and new discoveries had brought about the beginning of the industrial revolution in Europe even in the 15th and 16th centuries. This attraction towards scientific tendency in various fields of life had started in that every period but its application in the fields of education started only in the 17th and 18th centuries.

Impact of Science on the Ways of Life

The industrial and scientific revolutions he made had its impact on socio-economic life of the society as well. A new awakening was felt. People started giving up superstitions and other conservative beliefs. His theory of evolution had a great impact on the society. The facts of the values and beliefs were completely changed. People started thinking differently. They realized the importance of science ones religion and other superstition.

In this work on the proper sphere of Government (1842), he describes a scientific basis for the principles of right and wrong in conduct. In order to tell the meaning of moral conduct, he tells us, we must comprehend conduct as a whole, the conduct of all living creatures and the evolution of conduct and we must examine it in its physical, biological, psychological and social aspects. Spencer insists that the well being of the units and social groups and not the welfare of society as such is always the ultimate end of morality.

Spencer always argued against the modern socialist state. He holds the view that the all embracing state functions; He characterizes a low social type and its progress to a higher social type which is marked by the relinquishing of functions. He was committed to the laissez-faire theory in the social, economic and political spheres and believes that the general happiness can be realized only by letting individuals work out their own salvation, without undue interference by the state.

Spencer's Philosophy of Education

In his book entitled 'Education', Spencer criticized the education of the day. He said that it did not care to realize the importance either of the child or of the life and tries to catch things that could not be of practical value. He saw education as a typical impracticability. Children who were living in the worst possible circumstances were forced to appreciate beauty and learnt to appreciate it. It did not care to let them have any craft to enable them to live happily. He therefore suggested a new pattern of education which would bring about the following 5 types of activities.

- *(a)* Activities which help directly in the self preservation.
- *(b)* Those activities which are concerned with family life of children.
- *(c)* Those activities, which by securing the necessities of life-directly help in self preservation.
- *(d)* Social and political activities.
- *(e)* Leisure activities that are related to the gratification of the taste and feelings

Spencer opines that for a successful life, these activities are essential. Through education, the child should be taught to be able to perform these activities.

Importance of Teaching of Science

Spencer had laid stress on the teaching of science because he thought that only this education can equip a person to be able to live successfully. All the crafts of life are directly or indirectly related to mathematics, physics, chemistry etc. There is no such craft which does have a direct or indirect bearing to one of these. Science is capable of making a man self-dependant, hard working. Teaching of science is more valuable and stable than bookish knowledge. He says that when a man is able to probe into certain principles, on the basis of his own experiments, his reasoning power and capacity to analyze increases and, from the moral point of view, he is able to make progress.

Spencer and Aim of Education

According to Herbart Spencer, not to live in the material sense only, but in the wider sense. The general problem which comprehends every special problem in the right ruling of conduct in all directions, under all circumstances. To prepare us for complete living is the function which the education has to discharge.

Education, in the words of Herbart Spencer, has to equip us to be able to live complete. Education according to him should be able to equip the child to live completely, physically, intellectually, morally and socially. It was because of this that Spencer remarked, "Education must tell us what way to treat the body, in what way to treat the mind, in what way to manage our affairs, in what way to bring up the family, in what way to behave as a citizen."

Spencer and Curriculum

According to Herbart, "The idea of education is completely preparation of all these divisions. But failing this ideal; the aim should be to maintain a due proportion between the degrees of preparation in each, the greatest where the value is greatest, the less where the value is less, the least where the value is least."

Keeping in mind the aim of education complete living, he has recommended the inclusion of various subjects to help in all the activities. The subject to be taught, as suggested by Spencer, are

(a) For self presentation, physiology and hygiene should be taught. This will help the child to keep his body clean and save it from degeneration.
(b) For the activities that lead to the acquirement of the necessaries of life or for earning his livelihood, the child has to be taught language, arithmetic, geography and physical sciences.
(c) For the preservation of family and rearing of the children, teaching of domestic science, physiology and child psychology are necessary.
(d) For socio-political activities, history, sociology and economics are to be taught.
(e) For the activities of leisure, taste and feelings, literature, music, poetry and fine arts are to be taught.

These subjects have been categorized into useful and decorative or ornamental. Subjects falling under the 1st three groups are useful and the rest are decorative.

Spencer and Method of Teaching

Spencer laid emphasis on the mental and intellectual development of the child. He suggested certain teaching methods with this aim in view.

(a) Teaching should proceed from known to unknown.
(b) It should be from easy to difficult or from simple to complex.
(c) From direct to indirect should be the process through which teacher should proceed.
(d) From definite to indefinite should not be his approach as it is in the early step. On the other hand the teacher should start from indefinite to definite.
(e) The teacher should lead the child from the practical to the rational.
(f) The teaching of subjects should be in accordance with the 'Epoch theory of culture and emphasis should be on self-learning'.
(g) The students should be encouraged to make personal discoveries which helps in self-learning.
(h) The teaching should be pleasing and interesting.

Spencer's View to Physical Education

Spencer laid great stress on physical education. He was also of the view that 'a sound mind can be found only in a sound body'. He advocated a nutritive diet; the students should be permitted to line happily and not be scolded off and on. They should be acquainted with the rules of hygiene and good health. The curriculum also must provide for physical exercises.

Herbart Spencer's Contributions

Spencer had made a remarkable contribution to the field of education. Due to the impact of science as ways of life, a new awakening was felt. He was the first to release education from bondage of classical languages. He was well-versed with the views of Pestalozzi with regard to education and wrote various articles in it. In 1861, these articles were published in the form of a book 'Education'.

The first book written by him was 'Social Statics', 'First Principles' and 'The Origin of Species' became the center of a great battle of 'Books and this made Spencer the most famous philosopher of his time. First Principles was translated to most of the European languages and was adopted as a text book at oxford. The 1855 his second book 'The Principles of Psychology' undertook to trace the evolution of mind.

With sociology, the verdict in quite different. He wrote 'The Principles of Sociology regarding the problems of economics and government. Spencer was especially sensitive to the problem of finding a view and natural ethic to replace the moral code which had been associated with the traditional faith so he wrote 'The principles of ethics'.

Some other works are, 'Essays on the principles of morality', 'Various fragments', 'Facts and comments' and in his '*Autobiography*' he writes reviews his own early books, to show how it should have been done and he regards his Autobiography as the fondness of a father for a wayward son.

No doubt Spencer has given out to the world of education ideas, that are still honoured and respected, these ideas, in spite of all their importance, have certain drawbacks as well. Inspite of all the criticism, he made a remarkable contribution to the field of education.

He gave to philosophy a new contact with things and brought to it a realism which made German philosophy seem insignificant beside it. He summed up his age as no man had ever summed up any age and he accomplished so masterly a coordination of so vast an area of knowledge that criticism in almost shamed into silence by his achievement. We are standing at heights which his struggles and his labours won for us; we seem to be above him because he has raised us on his shoulders; some day, when the sting of his opposition in forgotten, we shall, do him better justice.

REFERENCES

1. Dash, B.N.—*A New Approach to Teacher & Education in the Emerging Indian Society*. Hyderabad: Neelkamal Publications Pvt. Ltd.
2. Russel, B. Wisdom of West. London Allen and Unwin.
3. Schofield, H. (1972). *The Philosophy of Education*. London: George Allen.
4. Sharma, Y.K.—*The Doctrines of the Great Indian Educators*. New Delhi: Kanishka Publishers, Distributors.
5. Sharma, Y.K.—*The Doctrines of the Great Western Educators from Plato to Bertrand Russell*. New Delhi: Kanishka Publishers, Distributors.
6. Sivarajan, K.—*Education in the Emerging Indian Society*. Calicut University, Central Co-Operative Stores.
7. Sodhi, T.S. *Philosophical Dimensions of Education*. Ambala: The Indian Publications.
8. Warnock, M. (1977). *Schools of Thought*. London: Faber and Faber.
9. Wynne. J.P. (1947). *Philosophies of Education*. London: Prentice Hall Inc.
10. www.wikipedia.com

15

Education and Social Stratification

"Man is not the creature of circumstances.
Circumstances are the creatures of men."

—*Disraeli*

A very important social phenomenon related with social stratification is the phenomenon of social mobility.

What is Stratification?

In the words of Young and Mack, "in most societies people classify one another into categories and rank these categories from higher to lower. The process of defining such categories is called "Social stratification and the resulting set of ranked categories is called the stratification structure." The categories themselves are called strata, popularly they are known as classes.

The rigidity of the stratification structure differs in different societies. In some it is extremely rigid while in others it is flexible. For example, the caste in India society is a very rigid stratification structure. Every member of a Hindu society is born into a category known as caste. He can never change his caste. His marriage has to take place within the caste bonds and to a great extent his profession is also decided by his caste affiliations.

There may be given three types of social characteristics used in stratification systems, considering the fullest spectrum of societies. These are: (1) such biologically grounded factors as: age, sex, race and kinship; (2) class characteristics such as occupation, wealth and power and (3) any number of idiosyncratic characteristics such as talent and personality. In any society the stratification may not be based on only any one of these criteria but two or more social characteristics may be mixed together.

Above stratification is described as leading to inequality or as a divisive force in the society. But this is only part of the picture. Stratification also serves as a cohesive social force. If it would have simply remained divisive all societies are doomed to destruction. Reissman believes that "the cohesive element in stratification derives primarily from the social values upon which it depends." The society has certain core beliefs. The stratification is due to the extension of these core beliefs. Thus the society's belief system finds an expression in the stratification process. Since the belief system is an unifying force the society becomes more cohesive through the stratification practiced by it. There are many ways in which the class structure of the society can be defined. Karl Marx used 'class' to mean persons having in common a specific relationship to the system of Economic production. Max Weber considered the stratification of societies on the basis of three variables: (1) the possession of economic goods and opportunities for income, (2) access to political power and (3) prestige or social honour. Warner considered a class as a number of people sharing a roughly equal level of prestige.

Education and Social Stratification

In Indian society stratification may be mentioned along three lines:

(a) Stratification on caste basis
(b) Stratification on religion basis and
(c) Stratification on economic class basis.

All the three aspects of stratification are more or less due to ascribed social positions. The religion and caste stratification is purely due to a person being born in a particular religious or caste group. The economic class distinctions are also based on positions at birth; however; changes are rapidly taking place in these types of ascribed positions. In Indian society the occupations are distributed on caste basis. Even now the scheduled castes by and large take up the same occupations as their forefathers, the Vaisha take up business and commerce and the Brahmins the learned professions. Since independence an inter caste mobility is visible. With the government incentives the members of the lower castes are taking up the vocations of the higher castes. But total impact of such movement is not very high and the society's occupations are still very much caste ridden.

Social Mobility

By "Social Mobility" Young and Mack mean movement within the social structure. When a person serving at a lower job moves to a job which provides him higher position and status he has altered his position in the class structure. The man can be described as socially mobile. One's class status is determined originally by the class status of his parents. When he achieves a different amount of education from that of his parents or moves into a different occupational stratum or adopts a different style of life he may be considered to be socially mobile. The term mobility is also used to the spatial movement or migration of a population. Such mobility occurs when the rural population migrate to urban areas or a section of population of one country migrates to another country.

Types of Mobility

Social Mobility may be of two types: (1) Vertical or (2) Horizontal. An alteration in status upward or downward is considered as indicative of vertical mobility. Horizontal mobility is movement from one status to another when there is no difference between the ranks of the two statuses. A person who is a farm labourer when becomes an industrial labourer has only moved horizontally. A son of sweeper when goes to the school, graduates and gets a high government job has moved upwards in status. This is an example of vertical mobility from the status position into which he was born.

Vertical mobility takes place whenever an individual's occupational status changes, his education level changes, his income undergoes change or his style of life's ranking in the stratification structure is altered. In sociological research a change in occupation is considered the best single indicator of social mobility. The reason for it is that occupational status is closely correlated with educational status, income, style of life and the other determinants of class status.

In the open society statuses are achieved and so there is great chance of vertical mobility. Education as one route to vertical mobility. It is through education that one can hope to replace the ascribed status by achieved status. It is through education alone that a sweeper's son can hope to rise to a level of government servant or to become a teacher, doctor or a magistrate.

The belief that upward mobility is both possible and desirable is called the 'mobility ethic'. This ethic is very clearly visible in the advanced countries while it is almost absent in the backward countries. Education can help in altering this situation. It may bring changes in the norms and the value-patterns. It can create a climate for hard work. Above all, education can crate a dissatisfaction with the status quo leading thereby to a desire to change one's status.

There may be described two important functions of the system of stratification. One is referred to as instrumental function—that of allocating persons to positions. The other is integrative function. This function is related to the individual's acceptance of their positions.

Education and Internal and External Constraints on Mobility

There are a number of factors which impede the vertical or horizontal mobility in a social structure. Here we are dealing with them as the constraints on mobility. These constraints may be internal or external. The internal constraints are values, aspirations and personality patterns of the individuals. The external constraints are the opportunity structure of a society and the structural settings with which the individual is influenced. The major constraint in the upward mobility is a system of beliefs and values prevailing in a social structure.

Family Influence

The mobility is also restricted due to the family influences. In a study by Stephenson it was found that both occupational plans and aspirations are positively associated with the prestige ranking of father's occupation.

Education here can play two-fold role: It can prepare all the individuals for vocations and thus crate a confidence in earning one's own living. The more stress it lays on women's education the more will it able to free the society from family bonds as women will gain confidence that they can also earn their living and are not dependent on near or distant relations and it can develop a desire for a better standard of life which can only be achieved by achieving higher positions. Thus people will look upward and will try to rise above the status positions of their families through a well organized system of education.

Factors in Individual's Personality

Very strong reasons for immobility may be found in an individual's personality structure. It has been found in a number of studies that achievement motivation, intelligence, aspirations and values are related with mobility.

REFERENCES

1. Soltis, J.F. (1968). An Introduction to the Analysis of Educational Concepts. London: Addison Wesla Publishers.
2. Tescond, C.A. & Morris, V. (1972). *The Antiman Culture: Bureau Technocracy and the Schools.* Urban University of Illinois Press.
3. Ulich, R. (1964). *Education and the Idea of Mankind.* New York: Harcourt Brace and World Inc.

16

Curriculum: Reforms, Construction and Evaluation

Introduction

What is curriculum? What is its purposes? How does it affect students and teachers? The way we define curriculum by and large reflects our approach to it. But the relationship between approach and definition is neither perfect nor mutually exclusive; approaches and definitions overlap.

Definition

A curriculum can be defined as a plan for action or a written document that includes strategies for achieving desired goals or ends. This position popularized by Ralph Tyler and Hilda Taba, exemplifies a linear view of curriculum. J. Galen Saylor; "Curriculum as a plan for providing sets of learning opportunities for persons to be educated."

Meaning of Curriculum

1. *Liberal Meaning:* The term curriculum is of Latin origin and it implies an athletic ground, thus indicating that curriculum is the ground through which the educand has to pass in order to reach a definite goal.
2. *Modern Interpretation:* Bent and Kronburg; "Curriculum, in its broadest sense. The complete school environment, involving all the courses, activities reading and associations furnished to the pupils in the school."
3. *Curriculum as Experience:* Munroc; "Curriculum embodies all the experience which are utilized by the school to attain the aims of education."

4. *Curriculum as a Means or Tool:* Cunningham; "The curriculum is the tool in the hands of the artist (the teacher) to mould his material (the pupil) according to his ideal (objective) in his studio (the school)."
5. *Curriculum as Environment*: H.L. Caswell; "The curriculum is all that goes on in the lives of the children, their parents and their teachers. The curriculum is made up of everything that surrounds the learner in all his working hours."
6. *Curriculum Includes all Activities*: H.H. Horne; "The curriculum is that which the pupil is taught. It involves more than the acts of learning and quiet study. It involves occupations, production, achievements, exercise, activity."
7. *Muthaliyar Commission (1952-53):* "Curriculum does not mean only the academic subjects traditional talk in the school but it includes the totality of experiences that people receives the manifold activities that go on in the school, in the classroom, library, lab, workshop, playgrounds and the numerous internal contacts between teachers and pupils." In this sense the whole life of the school becomes the curriculum, which can touch the life of schools at all points and help in the evolution of balanced personality.

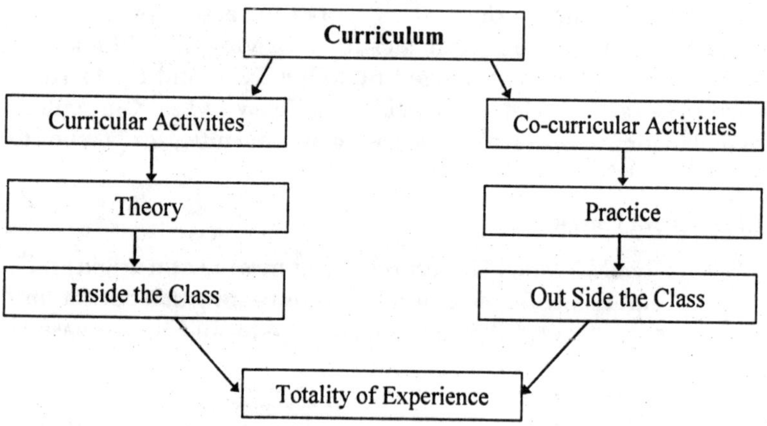

Curriculum = Syllabus + Co-curricular Activities

\+ Various aspects of Educational Environment

Characteristics of Curriculum

- Means to end
- Embodies totality
- Help in total development of children
- The best tool
- Attainment of objectives
- Effective link
- Dynamic
- Mirror of school
- Rounded whole knowledge

Foundations of Curriculum

- → Philosophical
- → Sociological
- → Psychological

Why Curriculum? Need and Importance of Curriculum

- Teachers true guide
- Attainment of objectives
- Systematic teachings
- Systematic presentation of knowledge
- Balancing curricular/co-curricular works
- Providers dynamism
- Teachers growth
- Examiners guide
- Course designers guide
- Democratic approach.

General Principles of Curriculum Construction

- The principle of child centeredness
- Activity orientedness
- Motivation
- Maturity
- Community centredness
- Creativity
- Elasticity and flexibility
- Balance
- Utility
- Comprehensiveness
- Preparation for life

- Training in the proper patterns of conduct
- Synthesis of play and work
- Synthesis of all activities of life
- Principle of individual differences
- Constant development
- Evolution of democratic values
- Variety.

Bases of Curriculum

The four bases of any curriculum are social forces, human development, the nature of learning and the nature of knowledge and cognition. All societies want to survive and progress. For this, they try to induct the young into their culture and values. School are very powerful agencies for this induction.

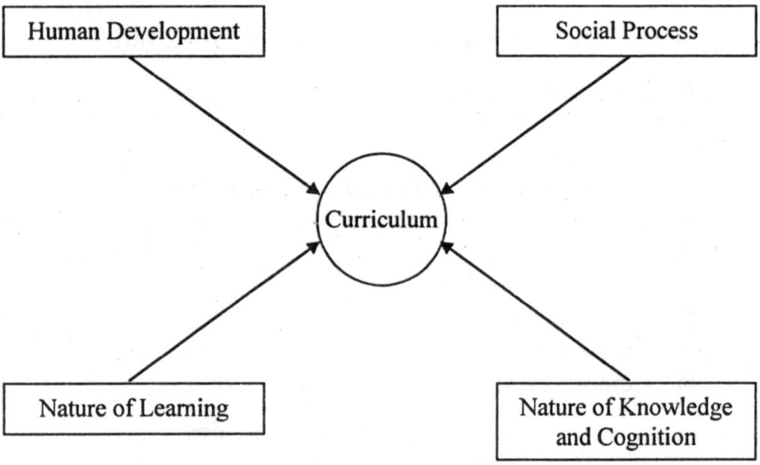

The Curriculum Process and its Stages

The curriculum process which can be divided into five stages. They are:

1. Selection of Aims, Goals and Objectives
2. Selection of Learning Experiences
3. Selection of Content
4. Organization and Integration of Learning Experiences and Content
5. Evaluation.

Major Approaches to Curriculum

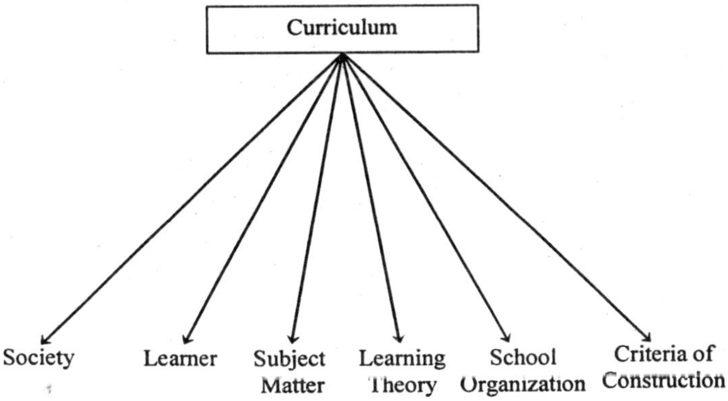

CURRICULAR REFORMS

Reform at the School Level

Among the lessons that can be deduced from past reform effort at the school level are the following developed by Ornstein and Levin.

1. *Adaptive Problem Solving*: Reform or innovation frequently has little or no effect on students because numerous problems arise to stifle practical application. E.g: Implementing of a new science curriculum.
2. *School Level Focus*: Because the innovating organization must identify and solve day to day problems, the focus in bringing about change must be at the level of the individual school building where many of the problems occur.
3. *Implementability*: Among the most important aspects of implementability are compatibility with the social context of potential users and accessibility to those who do not already understand or share the underlying ideas.
4. *Principal's Leadership*: Implementation requires change in many institutional arrangements, including scheduling of staff and student time, selection of utilization of instrumental methods and materials and mechanisms for making decisions. The building principal usually is the key person in successfully implementing change. In addition, the faculty must have a shared vision of the kinds of changes that are possible and necessary to improve their instructional programme.

5. *Teacher Involvement*: Because people who are expected to alter their working patterns will not co-operate fully unless they have a voice in designing and implementing charge, teachers must have an opportunity to select and evaluate innovations.
6. *Top-down and Bottom-up Approaches*: Since years of research had underlined the importance of teacher participation in decisions, researchers in the 1960's and 1970's, tended to emphasize a bottom-up approach in the change process in order to encourage a sense of ownership among teachers asked to devote much time and energy to implementing improvements in the 1980's tended to underline the importance of top down components in initiating change successfully.
7. *Staff Development*: Staff development is a core activity in the school improvement process, staff development to support improvement should be centered on the school as the basic unit not on the individual teacher.
8. *School Business Co-operation*: Many schools and school districts are attempting to improve the quality of education by co-operating with other institutions, particularly business and industry. Some of most promising programmes include 'partnership' or 'adopt-a-school' programmes in which a business and industry.

Finally the reform at the school level should involve five planning processes. Based on the results of 1,500 schools in New York state, the following principles emerge among reform and change-minded schools:

1. Curriculum change is ongoing and involves two essential ingredients, emphasis on basic skills and advanced level courses.
2. Research and evolution are priced; they use instruments to asses needs, plant improvements, and evaluate results.
3. Data are seriously considered, but the information is made clear, simple and brief before being presented.
4. Site-based collaboration is emphasis that is the staff is involved in planning and making decisions to ensure their commitment to change.
5. Instruction is emphasized while avoiding the tendency to be driven by test data or state wide assessments.

In short, these are five generic principles that school districts in all parts of the country can use as part of their mission pursuits or reform-change processes.

ORGANIZATION OF CURRICULUM AT ELEMENTARY AND SECONDARY STAGES

The main thrust areas of Indian education, as mentioned in the National Curriculum for Elementary and Secondary Education: A framework 1988, demand a fresh look. Some of the merit reformulation in the light of country's experience in the field of school education and the others have to be reaffirmed. Some new thrust areas may also need to be added in the light of the changes all round.

- Value education
- Common core components
- Toward an indigenous curriculum
- The minimum levels of learning
- Scheme of studies.

1. Early Childhood Education (ECE): Preparation for Primary Education (2 years)

This stage of education helps in preparing children for school and constitutes an important element of Early Childhood Care and Education (ECCE). It is available as a pre-school education component under Integrated Child Development Scheme (ICDS).

2. Elementary Education (8 years)/ Primary Stage (5 years)

Primary stage of education has been visualized in two segments with inherent internal continuity. The first segment comprises classes I and II where children are just introduced to formal teaching and at a stage of development which requires a smooth transition from informal and nonformal environment to a formal one.

The second segment consists of classes III-V where in the children get prepared to understand the environment and learn in a systematic way.

Curricular Areas at Different Stages

- Language that is, the three Language Formula,
- Mathematics
- Science and Technology
- Social Sciences

- Art of Healthy and Productive Living
- Work Education
- Art Education
- Health and Physical Education.

ORGANIZATION OF CURRICULUM OF HIGHER SECONDARY STAGE

After ten years of general education the higher secondary stage assumes great significance as students for the first time move toward diversification. Because,

- The stage of maximum challenge.
- Learners profile: A stage of transition from adolescence to youth.
- Access Equity and Excellence.
- Diversification and Flexibility.
- Semesterization.
- Credits.

Curriculum Organization

After the ten years common programme of studies, primarily of language skills, scientific literacy, basic mathematical and social skills, cultural heritage of the country, issues relating to political, economic and social life and environment. The stage is ripe for exposing the students to differentiated and specialized in depth courses in humanities, social sciences, science, mathematics, commerce, the like one hand and a variety of vocational courses on the others. Thus according to one of the most important recommendations of the Kothari commission, the curriculum at this stage is to be organized under two streams, the academic stream and the vocational stream; however there is a need to ensure that appropriate linkages between the two are not only maintained but systematically strengthened.

Academic Stream

Scheme of Studies: The curriculum at this stage will comprise,

1. *Foundation Courses*—Language, Work Education, Health and physical education.
2. *Elective Courses*—Modern Indian Languages and Literature, English, Foreign Languages, Science, Social Science Subjects, Commerce Subjects, Arts Subjects.

Instructional Strategy

- Training-cum production centres
- Integration of knowledge and skills
- Apprenticeship.

Open Learning System

Open learning system is increasingly becoming popular because of its capacity to provide education of comparable standards in a flexible and learner friendly manner, particularly to those who could not get access to the formal system of education obtaining within the country.

CURRICULUM DEVELOPMENT

Curriculum development means a continues or never ending process. Its outcome is known through students achievement of learning. Its assessment is made on the basis of change of behaviour of the learners.

The learning experiences provide desirable change of behaviour of the pupils. They are evaluated with the help of examination.

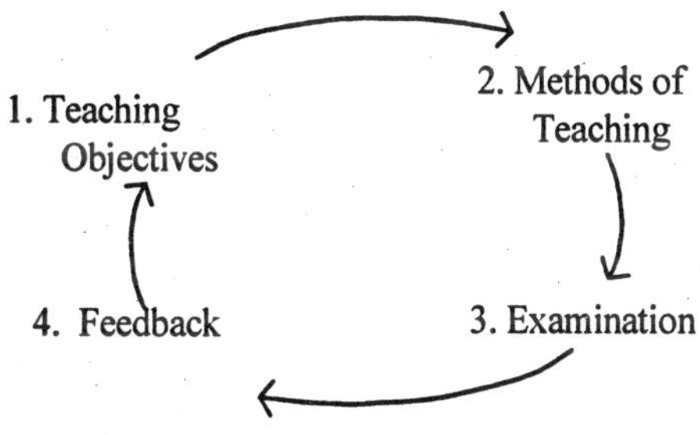

In curriculum development, the main focus of the curriculum is to develop the students. The curriculum is designed to realize the objective in terms of change of their behaviour. It is cyclic process.

1. Teaching objectives
2. Method of teaching
3. Examination
4. Feed Back.

Components of Curriculum Development

There are three components of educational process i.e., teacher, students and curriculum. It has three type of objectives- cognitive, affective and psychomotor. Educational process involves three major activities, teaching, training and instruction.

According to B.S. Bloom, it is a tripolar process (1) Educational objective, (2) Learning experiences and (3) Change of behaviour. It is cyclic process, shown in the following diagram.

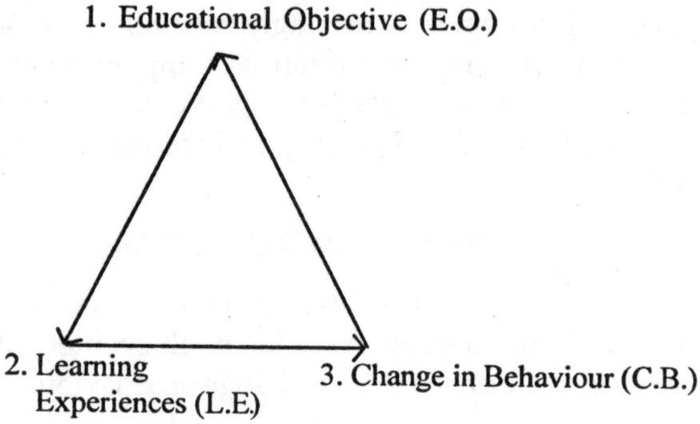

The teaching process is done through interaction between teacher and students. The curriculum is the basis for the interaction between teacher and taught.

Objectives of Curriculum Construction

1. Curriculum should provide the means for the alround development of a child. Teaching should be organized with the help of curriculum.
2. Curriculum must involve the human-experiences, culture and civilization which are to be transferred to new generation.
3. Curriculum should be the means to develop the moral character, discipline, honesty, co-operation, friendship, tolerance and sympathy with others.
4. Curriculum should help in developing the ability of thinking, wisdom, reasoning, judgement and other mental abilities.
5. It should consider the stages of growth and development of child for development attitude, interest, values and creative ability.
6. It should provide the awareness and understanding of physical and social environment and its components.
7. It should develop the right type of feeling and beliefs towards religious, new values and traditions.

8. It should help to develop democratic feeling and democratic way of life among students.
9. It should integrate the knowledge of various teaching subjects in view of their future life.
10. It should determine the mode of interaction between teacher and students in school. The mode of teaching is decided by the nature of curriculum.

Basic Elements of Curriculum Development

The educational process includes teaching, training and instructional activities. Teaching activities are performed by a teacher. They are planned or designed by the teacher according to four components.

1. Teaching-learning objectives
2. Teaching content or subject matter
3. Teaching method
4. Evaluation of learning outcomes.

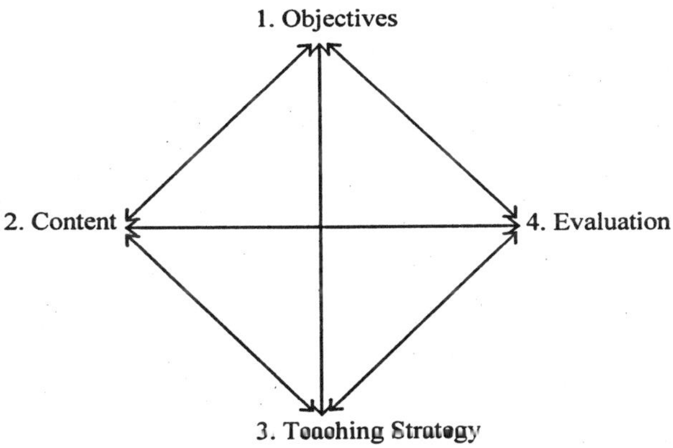

Transaction v/s Development of Curriculum

Curriculum Transaction	*Curriculum Development*
1. It is broad concept and area of curriculum.	1. It is a specific and narrow concept of curriculum.
2. Management of curriculum is done at initial stage of introduction of new courses at school stages and higher levels.	2. Curriculum development is a cyclic process used for improving and modifying the courses at particular state of level.

3. Management of curriculum employs the following steps 1. Planning 2. Organizing 3. Administering 4. Guiding 5. Controlling	3. It is a cyclic process using the following four steps. 1. Objectives 2. Instructional methods 3. Evaluation 4. Feed back

Models of Curriculum

Curriculum models are just as instructional designs. They bring competency in educational process and teaching learning. They are the best ways to proceed in formulating theories of teaching-learning. Instruction should begin with what is known about learning and instruction. Teaching models are the basis of teaching theories. The curriculum models are very useful for teachers for planning and organizing educational process. They can use models in the transaction of curriculum preparing an outline for guiding students activities and developing instructional procedure for realizing objectives. Curriculum models are very close to models of teaching. The following are the main models of curriculum.

1. Hilda Taba model of curriculum
2. Saran model of curriculum
3. Mukhopadhaya model of curriculum.

Administrative Model of Curriculum Development

Management refers to conscious performance from variety of alternative plus proposals and further the more that such choices involve purposeful commitment to recognize and derive objectives. Management employs strategies to achieve the objectives.

It indicates the various activities performed under the development of curriculum.

1. Planning a curriculum
2. Formulating Educational Objectives
3. Organizing the Tasks
4. Employing Strategies and Techniques
5. Selecting and Appointing Workers
6. Executing and Co-ordinating Among Workers
7. Evaluating and Controlling the Tasks
8. Encouraging and Providing Feedback.

Administrative model is related to management technology. Its broad outline is developed under 'instruction design'. The basis of 'management' involves the following five activities. (1) Planning, (2) Organization, (3) Administration or Execution, (4) Guiding, (5) Controlling of Feedback.

Education is a system which was various sub-systems. It is assumed that no system is perfect. Every system or sub-system needs improvement or development. The term "curriculum development" refers to the improvement in the curriculum.

I.K. Devies has designed and introduced "Managing Teaching Learning Approach" which involves four steps in educational process.

1. Planning of Teaching
2. Organizing Teaching
3. Learning of Teaching
4. Controlling Teaching.

The last step known as 'controlling teaching' means evaluation of objectives which provide the feedback for improving these steps. The planning includes managing curriculum and implementing curriculum. The basic model of curriculum depends on the objectives of education.

Bases of Development of Curriculum

The development of curriculum is the commitment for realizing desired objectives of education. The objectives are based on various consideration and factors. The same considerations are equally important in planning or deciding the basic structure of curriculum. The following are the bases of transaction of curriculum.

1. Social philosophy of the society.
2. National needs or state needs.
3. Nature of course of study.
4. Type of examination system.
5. Form of the government.
6. Theory of assumptions of human organization.
7. Growth and development stage of students.
8. Recommendations of national commissions and committee of education.

The above basis of curriculum management and educational objectives are theoretical and practical. The last basis is more practical in transaction of curriculum. After independence several commissions and committees have been established in Education-University Education Commission (1949), Secondary Education Commission (1952), National Commission of Education (1964-66) and National Policy of Education (1986) etc. These commissions have given the recommendations for managing curriculum or course of study for different stages.

SYSTEM ANALYSIS MODEL OF CONSTRUCTION AND DEVELOPMENT OF CURRICULUM

System analysis is closely related to both training psychology and cybernetic. It has emerged during second world war. It has greatly influenced management decision making in business, industry, government and military. Known by several terms, system analysis had gained considerable standardization.

Meaning of System Analysis

The word system has been derived from the field of engineering. A system is the sum total of agents working independently and dependently together to achieve the required goals. The term 'system' conveys the meaning of analysis and development.

System technology brings to educational management a scientific-quantitative approach for solving complex educational administrative problems.

Procedure of System Analysis

The following steps must be utilized for conducting system analysis study:

1. First step: Formulation of Objectives
2. Second step: Review of System Operation
3. Third step: Collection of Data
4. Fourth step: Analysis of Data
5. Fifth step: Isolation of the Problem
6. Sixth step: Specify operations in the problem
7. Seventh step: Block diagram.

Procedure of System Analysis

(System Analysis Chart)

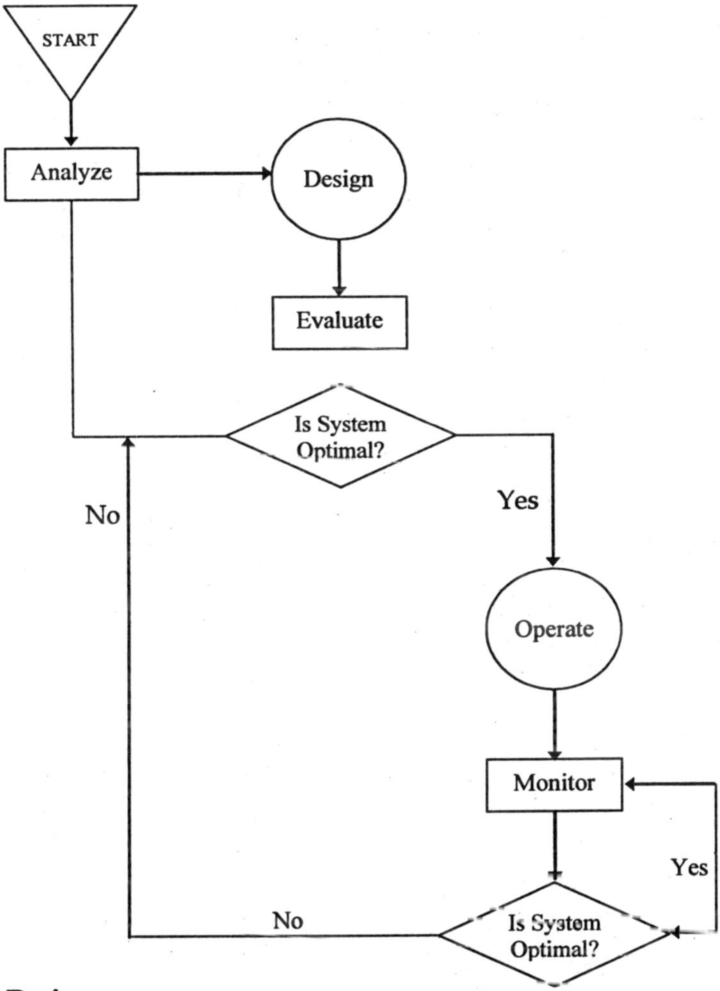

Design

After the system analysis, the investigator attempts to design and tentative solution of the problem. A new solution of the problem is subjected to testing. A tentative solution and re-testing the tentative solution continues until an analyst reaches to an optimal solution. Once optimal solution is obtained, the analyst departs that loop.

Evaluation

The formal evaluation of the new solution is made for checking out its workability. It involves implementation of tentative solution in some aspect of the system. It is advisable to evaluate all new system solutions in small scale of the required operations.

System Operations

The new design has been implemented within the system for formal evaluation and acceptance for the solution of the problem. It involves two aspects.

1. Implementation of new system operation.
2. Maintenance of the system where a new system is designed.

Criteria for Evaluating System Analysis Project

1. Performance
2. Cost
3. Utility
4. Time.

Application of System Analysis in Education

The purpose of the system analysis is to get the 'Best environment on the best place for the best people of the best time and in the best price'.

The educational implication of system analysis have been found in the following areas of education.

1. Approach
2. Problems
3. Training
4. Sub-systems
5. Change.

System Approach

System approach is a rational, problem solving method of analyzing the educational process and making it more effective. System is the process taken as a whole incorporating of all its aspects and parts namely pupils, teachers, curriculum content, instructional materials, instructional strategies, physical environment and the evaluation of instructional objectives.

Keshaw and Michean (1959); "System approach is one of the techniques which aims at finding the most efficient and economically intelligent methods for solving the problems of education scientifically."

The system concept provides a frame work for visualizing internal and external environmental factors as an integrated whole.

CURRICULUM EVALUATION

1. Formative Curriculum Evaluation

Formal assessment made in a situation when the curriculum is answerable to the public. Assessment in such a situation must ensure objectivity, credibility and relevance. To ensure these, it will follow the get standardized norms/procedures of test construction, administration and interpretation. Informal assessment is applicable to situations where an individual or a voluntary body is a curriculum to obtain some information to fulfill some personal requirements. The informal assessment also needs to be objective and reliable, but the evaluator is not bound to satisfy about these qualities of his assessment. Hence, the process of assessment need not follow the set procedures of evaluation.

2. Summative Assessment

Formative assessment is concerned with identifying learner weakness in attainment in order to help the learner and the teacher overcome/remedy those summative aims at certifying and grading the attainment of the learner at the end of a given course.

(i) Test, for formative assessment are given at regular and frequent intervals during a course, while the tests for summative assessment are given at the end of a course or at the end of a fairly long period, say a term or a semester or a year. In a course that extends over six months, a test at the end of say, every fortnight will be a formative test, while the test at the end of the six months will be summative.

(ii) The level of generalization sought by the items of a summative test will be much higher compared to that sought by the items of a formative test. For instance if the items of a formative test check the ability to apply a given rule or principle to a given unfamiliar situation, the items in a

summative test may check the ability to apply one or more to the appropriate rules/principles from among the many given in a variety of situations.

(iii) The formative assessment includes tests and other forms of measurement intended to give a measure of success of the parts of a curriculum even when the curriculum is in the process of development. Summative evaluation includes such form of measurement that would give a measure of success of the course as a whole.

3. Developmental Assessment

'Developmental Assessment' used in the context of curriculum development, it refers to the evaluation of the preliminary versions of curriculum with representative sample of learners. It is generally treated as a part of the curriculum development schedule. Formative evaluation in this context refers to the evaluation of a course made with larger group of learners. The purpose of such assessment is not to help the process of curriculum development but to help the activities of maintenance and revision of curriculum already developed.

Criteria for Curriculum Evaluation

There are four major criteria for assessing the workability of the curriculum.

1. *Subject-Content*: Various subjects are included in the curriculum. The structure and content of these subjects is determined for the curriculum development.
2. *Experiences:* The curriculum provides the social, historical, political, geographical, physical, civic senses, religious, spiritual and reactive experiences, expression of ideas facts and events.
3. *Skills*: Curriculum provides the situations for developing skills or psychomotor activities- related to psychomotor objectives.
4. *Attitude and Values*: Curriculum provides the experiences for developing affective domain of the learners.

Related to cognitive, affective and psychomotor domains the factors are given due weightage in good curriculum.

Interpretation of Evaluation Results

Evaluation results are interpreted in various ways from different said prints and for different purposes such as guidance, performance etc.

Conclusion

Let us concluding by the words of Cunningham; "Curriculum is the tool in the hands of the artist (the teacher) to mould his material (the pupil) according to his ideal (objective) in his studio (school).

REFERENCES

1. IGNOU (2002). *Curriculum Planning*. New Delhi: IGNOU.
2. Khan, M.I. & Nigam, B.K. (1993). *Evaluation and Research in Curriculum Construction*. New Delhi: Kanishka Publishers, Distributors.
3. Morrison, G.S. (1993). *Contemporary Curriculum*. USA: Allyn & Bacon.
4. NCERT (2000). *National Curriculum Frame Work for School Education*. New Delhi: NCERT.
5. Ornstein, A.C. & Hunkins, F. (1993). *Curriculum-Foundations Principles and Theory, 2nd Edn*. USA: Allyn & Bacon.
6. Prasad, J. & Kaushik, V.K. (1997). *Advanced Curriculum Construction*. New Delhi: Kanishka Publishers, Distributors.
7. UGC (1991). *Report of the Curricular Development Centre in Education*. New Delhi: UGC.

Bibliography

Apple, M. (1979). *Ideology and Curriculum*. Boston: Routledge and Regan Paul.

Arnstine, D. (1967). *Philosophy of Education: Learning and Schooling*. New York: Harper & Row, 1967.

B.N. Dash- *A New Approach to Teacher & Education in the Emerging Indian Society*. Hyderabad: Neelkamal Publications Pvt. Ltd.

Barrow, R. (1966). *Radical Education*. New York: Harper & Row.

Belock & Green J.L. (Eds.). *Philosophy and Education*. Meerut: Any Prakashan.

Bowen, J. (1971). *A History of Western Education, Vol. 2*. London: Methuen & Co.

Boyd, W. (Revised by King E.J.) (1964). *The History of Western Education*. London: Adam & Charles Black.

Brameld, T. (1956). *Towards a Reconstructed Philosophy of Education*. New York: Dryden Press.

Brameld, T. (1961). *Education for the Emerging Age (Newer Ends & Stronger Means)*. New York: Harper & Row.

Brameld, T. (1971). *Patterns of Educational Philosophy*. New York: Hold Rinehart & Winston.

Broudy, H.S. (1977). *Building a Philosophy of Education*. New York: Krieger.

Brown, L.M., (1970). *Aims of Education*. New York: Teachers' College Press.

Brubacher, J.S. (Ed.) (1955). *Philosophies of Education Forty-first Year Book NSSE Part I*. Chicago: University of Chicago Press.

Brubacher, J.S. (Ed.). (1955). *Modern Philosophies of Education 54th Year Book, NSSE*. Chicago University Press.

Bruhacher, J.S. (1974). *A History of Problems of Education*. London: McGraw Hill.

Butler, *Four Philosophies of Education*.

Butler, J.D. (1966). *Idealism in Education,* New York, Harper and Row.

Butts, R.F. (1947). *A Culture History of Education.* London: Mc Graw Hill.

Chamberline, J.G. (1969). *Toward a Phenomenology of Education.* Philadelphia: Westminster Press.

Curtis, S.J. & Boultwood, M.E.A. (1953). *A Short History of Educational Ideas.* London: University Tutorial Press.

Dearden, R.F., Hirst. P.H. Peters, R.S. (Eds.). *A Critique of Current Educational Aims.* Boston: Routledge & Kegan Paul, 1972.

Denton, D.E. (Ed.). (1974). *Existentialism and Phenomenology in Education.* New York: Teachers' College Press.

Dewey, J. (1916). *Democracy and Education.* New York: MacMillan.

Doyle, J. (1973). *Educational Judgements.* London: Routledge & Kegan Paul.

Dupuis, A.M. (1966). *Philosophy of Education Historical Perspective.* New York: Ran McNally.

East Hope, G. (1975). *Community Hierarchy & Open Education.* London: Routledge & Kegan Paul.

Eby, F. (1952). *The Development of Modern Education.* New York: Prentice Hall.

Elvin, L. (1977). *The Place of Commonsense in Educational Thought.* London: George Allen & Unwin, 1977.

Ferry, L.R. (1967). *Four Progressive Education*: B. Russel, A.S. Neil, H. Loul, E.H. Kilpatrick. New York: MacMillan.

Freire, P. (1874). *Education for Critical Consciousness.* New York: Seabury Press.

Freire, P. (1970). *Pedagogy of the Oppressed.* New York. Herder & Herder.

Freire, P. (1976). *Education: The Practice of Freedom.* London: Writers and Readers.

Frost, S.E. (Jr.) (1966). *Historical and Philosophical Foundations of Western Education.* Ohio, Charles E. Merrill.

Goodman, P. (1964). *Compulsory Miseducation.* New York: Horizon Press.

Government of India (1948). *University Education Commission.*

Government of India (1956). *Secondary Education Commission Report.*

Government of India (1962-64). *Education and National Development.*

Government of India (1986). *New Policy on Education.*

Graves, F.P. (1937). *A History of Education Before the Middle Ages.* New York: Macmillan Co.

Hart, J.K. (1935). *Education for an Age of Power.* New York: Harper & Brothers.

Hirst, H. (1974). *Knowledge and the Curriculum: A Collection of Philosophical Papers.* London: Routledge & Kegan Paul, 1974.

Hocking, W.E. (1938). *Types of Philosophy.* New York: Charles Scribuses Sons.

Hughes, A.G., Hughe, E.H. (1960). *Education: Some Fundamental Problems.* London: ELBS & Longmans Green and Co., 1960.

Illich, I. (1971). *Deschooling Society.* New York: Harper & Row.

Joshi, K. (1975). *Education for Personality Development.* New Delhi: N.C.E.R.T.

Kabir, H. (1955). *Science, Democracy and Islam,* London: Allen & Unwin.

Kilpatric, W.H. (1951). *Philosophy of Education.* New York: The Macmillan Co.

Kneller, G.F. (1971). *Introduction to the Philosophy of Education.* New York: John Willy & Sons, 1971.

Lawrence, E. (1970). *The Origin and Growth of Modern Education.* Baltimore: Penguin.

Longford, G. & O. Connor, D.J. (1973). *New Essays in the Philosophy of Education.* London: Routledge & Kegan Paul.

Lucas, J.C. (1972). *Our Western Educational Heritage.* New York: MacMillan.

Mann, J.H. *Learning to be: The Education of Human Potential.* New York: Free Press.

Martin, W.O. (1969). Realism in Education. New York: Harper & Row.

Maslow, A.H. (Ed.) (1959). *New Knowledge in Human Values.* London: Harper & Row.

Mayee, J.B. (1971). Philosophical Analysis in Education. New York: Harper & Row.

Mayer, F. (1964). *A History of Educational Thought.* Columbus, Charles E. Merritl.

Mc Clellan, J.E. (1971). *Philosophy of Education.* New Jersey: Prentice Hall Inc.

McDermott J.J. (Ed.). *The Philosophy of John Dewey Vol. 2.* New York: Putnam.

Mohanty, J. (1982). *Indian Education in the Emerging Society,* New Delhi: Sterling.

Monroe, Paul. (2001). *Encyclopaedia of Philosophy of Education.* New Delhi: Cosmo Publications.

Moore, T.W. (1974). *Educational Theory: An Introduction.* Boston: Rentledge & Kegan Paul.

Morris, V. (1966). *Existentialism in Education*. New York Harper & Row.

Morrish, I. (1967). *Disciplines of Education: Philosophy of Plato, Rousseau, Deway Psychology; Freud Piaget Skinner, Sociology: Derkheim, Mannheim, Mead*. London:Allen & Unwin.

Nakosteen, M. (1968). *History of Islamic Organize of Western Education*. Roulder: University of Colorado Press.

Narvane. V.S. (1978). *Modern Indian Thought*. New Delhi, Orient Longman Ltd.

O'Connor, D.J. (1957). *An Introduction to the Philosophy of Education*. London: Routledge Kegan Paul.

Painter, F.V.N. (Ed.). (1905). *Great Pedagogical Essays: Plato to Spencer*. New York: American Book Co.

Paratte, R. (1977). *Ideology and Education*. New York Mcday.

Patel, M.S. (1953). *Educational Philosophy of Mahatma Gandhi*. Ahamadabad: Navajivan.

Percy, Nunn. (1960). *Education its Data and First Principle*. London: Edward Arnold Ltd.

Peters, R.S. (1963). *Authority Responsibility and Education*. London: George Allen & Unwin.

Power. E.J. (1969). *Evolution of Educational Doctrine Major Educational Theorists of the Western World*. New York: Appleton-Century-Crofts.

Price, K. (Ed.) (1962). *Education and Philosophical Thought*. Boston: Allyn & Bacon.

Radhakrishnan, S. & Moore. *Source Book of Indian Philosophy*. Allen & Uncoin.

Reid, L.A. (1962). *Philosophy and Education*. London: Heinsmann.

Rena, R. (1971). *Introduction to Indian Philosophy*. New Delhi: Tata Mac Graw Hill.

Roman, F.W. (1930). *The New Education in Europe*. London: Routledge & Sons.

Ross, J.S. (1960). *Ground-Work of Education Theory*. London: George G. Harrap & Co. Ltd.

Rudy, W. (1965). *School in an Age of Mass Culture*. New York: Prentice Hall.

Rusk R. Robert. (1951). *A History of Indian Education*. London: University of London Press.

Russel L. Hamm. (1981). *Philosophy and Education: Alternatives in Theory and Practice*. Illinois: The Inter State Printers & Publishers, Inc.

Russel, B. (1972). *Education and the God Life*. New York: Leverlight.

Russel, B. Wisdom of West. London Allen and Unwin.

Russell, B. (1947). *History of Western Philosophy*. London: George Allen and Unwin.

Sarup, M. (1978). *Marxism and Education*. Boston: Routledge & Kegan Paul.

Schofield, H. (1972). *The Philosophy of Education*. London: George Allen & Unwin.

Sharma, Ram Nath. (2000).*Textbook of Educational Philosophy*. New Delhi: Kanishka Publishers, Distributors.

Sharma, Y.K.—*The Doctrines of the Great Indian Educators*. New Delhi: Kanishka Publishers, Distributors.

Sharma, Y.K.—*The Doctrines of the Great Western Educators From Plato to Bertrand Russell*. New Delhi: Kanishka Publishers, Distributors.

Sivarajan, K.—Education in the Emerging Indian Society. Calicut University,Central Co-Operative Stores.

Sodhi, T.S. *Philosophical Dimensions of Education*. Ambala: The Indian Publications.

Soltis, J.B. (Ed.). *Philosophy of Education Since Midcentury*. New York: Teachers' College Press.

Soltis, J.F. (1968). *An Introduction to the Analysis of Educational Concepts*. London: Addison Wesla Pub.

Soltis, J.F. (Ed.). (1981). *Philosophy and Education, Eightieth Year Book of MSSE*. Chicago: University of Chicago Press.

Tagore, R. (1922). *Creative Unity*. New Delhi: Macmillan.

Tescond, C.A. & Morris, V. (1972). The Antiman Culture: Bureau Technocracy & the Schools, Urban University of Illionois Press, 1972.

Thut, I.W. (1967). *The Study of Education*. New York: McGraw Hill, 1967.

Ulich, R. (1964). *Education and The Idea of Mankind*. New York: Harcourt Brace & World Inc.

Ulich, R. (1947). *Three Thousand Years of Educational Wisdom*. Cambridge: Harvard University Press.

Vanderberg, D. (1971). *Being and Education: An Essay in Existing Phenomenology*. Englewood Cliff. New Jersey: Prentice-Hall.

Vivekananda (1982). *Complete Works of Swami Vivekananda, Vol. V*. Advits Publishers.

Warnock, M. (1977). *Schools of Thought*. London: Faber and Faber.

Whitehead, A.N. (1929). *The Aims of Education and Other Essays*. New York: Free Press.

Wingo, G.M. (1974). *Philosophies of Education: An Introduction*. New Delhi: Sterling.

www.wikipedia.com

Wynne. J.P. (1947). *Philosophies of Education*. London: Prentice-Hall Inc.

Index